DEVELOPING ARTISTIC AND PERCEPTUAL AWARENESS

BROWN

ART SERIES

Edited by

WILLARD F. WANKELMAN
Bowling Green State University
Bowling Green, Ohio

DEVELOPING ARTISTIC AND PERCEPTUAL AWARENESS

art practice in the elementary classroom

Earl W. Linderman and Donald W. Herberholz

Department of Art • *Sacramento State College* • *California*

WM. C. BROWN COMPANY PUBLISHERS

135 SOUTH LOCUST STREET • DUBUQUE, IOWA 52003

Manufactured by WM. C. BROWN CO. INC., Dubuque, Iowa
Printed in U. S. A.

"I am certain of nothing but the holiness of the heart's affections and the truth of imagination—what the imagination seizes as beauty must be truth whether it existed before or not."

Letter to
Benjamin Bailey from John Keats,
November 22, 1817.

Foreword

Modern life with all of its complexities and all of its abstractions seems to add a bar each day of our lives so that, like canaries, we are in danger of becoming prisoners of life. It is only the wise and the persistent who flee regularly from their cages to touch the real earth through a direct experience, coming face to face with nature, face to face with fellow men, or face to face with a simple lump of clay. It is in this direct experience that man is called upon to use his own thoughts, feelings and actions. Regardless of the simplicity of the experience, the individual must construct responses in his own way. What most of us take for granted as a normal pattern of growth is in reality a series of most serious struggles which go on within every individual. Growth implies change and change can be frightening. Even mature artists sometimes admit to a real fear when faced with the emptiness, the challenge of a blank canvas; for standing alone, unassisted, the individual is now entirely dependent upon his own resources—energy and motivation must create the answers which are his truths.

When one can stand apart from a group of children engaged in their creative activities and single out any one of the group for detailed observation, objectively analysing behavior, working habits, sequences of actions and responses, ability or inability to perceive, and interactions, one begins to sense, if only in a small way, the problems and frustrations of growth and change. For many years educators have had the benefit of the experience of inspiring, intuitive teachers like Cizek and Cole and brilliant scholars like Lowenfeld, Read, and Arnheim who have coupled research with intuition. More recently, younger scholars like Beittel, Barkan, McFee, Burkhart and others have supplied additional information and insight into the nature of child art and learning in the arts. Many of their insights are such that simple verbalization rarely explains them and there are, of course, dangers inherent in only synoptic adoption of insights. Sometimes those things which are most meaningful to one may be lost on a follower unless it is possible to reach the same depth of under-standing and to work under similar conditions. How futile it would be to ape Cizek whose culture environment and children differed so greatly from ours. Mr. Linderman, Mr. Heberholz, and I agree that each teacher must create his own rich environ-ment to nurture the creative potential of his flock.

This book presents an open condition in which a multitude of findings are laid bare before the reader and gives original sources of much inspired thought. Digging deeper helps us elude the danger of oversimplification in one of the most important facets of the child's growth—his creative development. More important here, however, is the feeling of excitement which rubs off onto the reader the minute the pages are turned. Clearly, the class-room teacher is expected to teach, and to teach in an inspired way. The factor of chance is hardly considered a worthy approach in education. Art education has suffered occasionally through the casualness of chance success, in many cases by the mere misunderstanding of the relationship between the child's art product and the process of making it. The common misinterpre-tation of process vs. product, particularly at the elementary school level, has led to all kinds of perversions of a most important and meaningful concept. Teachers have sometimes adopted the notion that anything a child does is both good and acceptable. I watched a class being taught one day in which the teacher walked through the group lifting every piece and gushing oohs and aahs in the most public sort of way. Any scratch or blob was loudly praised for its freshness, vitality or spontaneity. As I watched, I noticed one small boy who had caught on to the fact that the teacher praised indiscriminately. Playfully turning his back to his paper, and with a loaded brush, he proceeded to slosh the paper heavily. As he anticipated, his paper warranted a fair share of high praise. This created a dilemma, for the teacher was right in wanting to encourage each child and yet as she was discovered to be praising everything indiscriminately, she was losing the confidence of her students. The accidental paper of the little boy may have been aesthetically the most pleasing piece in the class, but the mere fact that the child sensed in-sincerity in the teacher was most damaging.

The notion of process and product might better be thought of as inseparable. A weak product is merely a record of a poor process, which in turn may be the result of diffuse motivation. On the other hand, a good product is the record of a strong period of process and high motivation. This whole matter is further complicated by the fact that the teacher is expected to be a skilled and mature person whose job it is to assist each child to attain levels of achievement that he might not otherwise reach. Everyone who has taught recognizes the fact that children are sometimes so highly motivated that the teacher seems only to be in the way. But left only to his own resources, the child may reach a plateau from which he can no longer seem to ascend. It is here that the sensitive teacher guides, suggests, and stimu-lates the child so that his spark of desire is reignited and he is challenged and aided in his desire to seek new solutions. Once renewed, he goes on to achieve new levels of accomplishment. All this is tied up with the matter of growth which is some-times falsely considered to be an automatic part of the years in school. It is easy to deceive oneself into believing that, by merely having a few token art lessons, the child will pass smoothly through the various developmental levels which are recognized by most art educators. This, in part, is so, but what happens is that the child may pass through each level with the weakest kinds of concepts, failing to lay the necessary foundations for the stages which follow. Ultimately his concepts become so weak and insignifiant the child loses confidence in them and thus rejects his own means of expression and communication. Growth and change are difficult for the child, and successful growth is very dependent upon teachers who care, or perhaps I should say teachers "who care to give the very best."

Some years ago I began a collection of virtually all of the drawings and paintings of a single child in order to try to determine the manner in which concepts change. This collection grew until it amounted to thousands of drawings and paintings. The various stages of development were clearly evident, but a study of all of the drawings in chronological order revealed many clues to the struggles of growth. During the period around six years of age the child developed over thirty different kinds of noses for his people, trying to arrive at a concept that would satisfy him. This was not a steady progression, but rather an irregular moving forward with a periodical return to older symbols, an occasional modification, and a sudden new surge forward. I began to see what hard work it was to be involved in all of these discoveries. Occasionally an enormous forward thrust appeared which resulted from increased perceptual awareness, no doubt brought about by a sensitive teacher who had provided a good experience or stimulation. How important it was that the teacher found the means to help the child remain open and receptive as well as flexible in his approach. These are characteristics which will serve him well throughout all of life's activities. The teacher finds himself frequently walking a tightrope to maintain a balance between too easily satisfied children and those who are too quickly dissatisfied.

One of the conditions of achieving the full potential of every child is a sustained program of opportunities with the presence of materials and equipment and circumstances necessary for performance. The child must have the opportunity to fully explore his abilities, for no potential will ever be realized, or even be discovered, unless a child tries an activity and freely participates. As teachers, we receive the finest kind of raw material. When one considers the potential of a simple chunk of coal which can be turned into any of thousands of products, one is staggered by the potential of a classroom full of children. Most children come with an openness, ready to absorb the stuff of education. The tiny child is all perception; tasting, touching, seeing, smelling, hearing and asking. The most formidable task of education is to keep this perception open and to help it develop both sensitivity and selectivity.

Life cannot absorb everything indiscriminately, for ultimately life takes on direction and focus. Such a challenge requires teachers who care deeply and teachers who regard teaching as a great adventure of the human spirit. The authors of this book, Earl Linderman and Donald Herberholz, are creative artists who have sought their own personal truths in both artistic production and creative teaching. They recognize that what is "right" is an elusive something that each teacher must seek and find for himself. This search requires a grasp of fundamental concepts plus the teacher's own intuition. All of this does not suggest any radical reorganization of the programs of the classroom, it simply suggests a means to a richer environment in which creative growth can take place through greater awareness and greater sensitivity.

Edward L. Mattil
Chairman, Department of Art Education
Pennsylvania State University

January, 1964.

Acknowledgments

The authors wish to thank the following organizations and individuals for permission to quote:

The American Crayon Company for the quotation from "Everyday Art" by Yar G. Chomicky.

Art Education: Journal of the National Art Education Association for a quotation by Howard Conant from a symposium held at the Philadelphia Museum College of Art on Dec. 11, 1962.

Arts and Activities for quotations from "Let's Learn about Art" by Earl W. Linderman.

Crocker Art Gallery and *Everyday Art Magazine* for photographs. All photographs are by the authors unless otherwise noted.

Davis Publications, Inc., for quotations from "Art Activities for the Very Young" by F. Louis Hoover and "Painting in the Classroom" by Arne W. Randall and Ruth Elise Halvorsen.

Grade Teacher for "Child Art and the Teacher" by Earl W. Linderman.

Harper & Brothers for quotations from "Creativity and its Cultivation" edited by Harold Anderson.

Houghton Mifflin Company for the quotation from "The Natural Way to Draw" by Kimon Nicolaides.

International Textbook Co. for quotations from "Spontaneous and Deliberate Ways of Learning" by Robert C. Burkhart and "Art: Search and Self-Discovery" by James A. Schinneller.

J. B. Lippincott Co. for the quotation from "The Art Spirit" by Robert Henri.

The Macmillan Company for quotations from "Your Child and His Art" and "Creative and Mental Growth" by Viktor Lowenfeld.

New York State College of Home Economics for the quotation from "Children's Art" by W. Lambert Brittain in the Cornell Extension Bulletin, 1067.

Pantheon Books, Inc., for the quotation from "Education through Art" by Herbert Read.

Prentice-Hall, Inc., for the quotation from "Meaning in Crafts" by Edward L. Mattil.

The Ronald Press Company for the quotation from "A Foundation for Art Education" by Manuel Barkan.

Saturday Review for the quotation from "What Makes a Person Creative" by Donald W. MacKinnon.

Scientific American for the quotation from "Psychology of Imagination" by Frank Barron.

Syracuse University Press for the quotation from "Creativity and Psychological Health" by Michael F. Andrews.

Vision for the quotation from "Seeing Things" by Arthur Syverson.

Wadsworth Publishing Co., Inc., for quotations from "Preparation for Art" by June King McFee and "Creativity: Invitations and Instances" by Alice Miel et al.

The authors wish also to express their gratitude to their wives, Marlene Linderman and Barbara Heberholz, for their entire understanding and help during the creation of this book.

Introduction

In a highly standardized, mechanistic society loss of human rights and dignities is threatened by a lack of the individual's opportunities to create. Individual innovation is being replaced by a national mass-mediocre-mindedness. Man is being stripped of many of his powers to perceive, imagine, explore, and invent. The loss of this ability can be overcome through the exercising of the individual sensibilities and the seeking of basic principles through a creative search. The ideas contained in this book are intended to amplify the creative individualism of man and to "sense art's overwhelming power, the near-blinding beauty of its white-hot, aesthetic core"[1] through a depth of experiences in art practices.

This guide is written to help teachers and parents stimulate in children experiences which are basic to a rich unfolding of their creative expression. The ideas contained in this book are not merely theoretical but have resulted from carefully reasoned insights gained through successful teaching experiences with children. In addition, evidence based on ex-

---

[1]Quote by Howard Conant, as reported in *Art Education, Journal of the National Art Education Association*, from a symposium held at the Philadelphia Museum College of Art on December 11, 1962.

tensive scientific research done in the fields of child psychology and art education form the nucleus of this presentation.

This book is especially designed to help the parent or teacher to experience once again the beauty of life through fresh eyes. This fresh vision in experiencing the world will be an aid in teaching children an appreciation of its wonders and beauties. Children will learn to discover their own aesthetic and artistic imagery when they learn to open the magic door of their awareness and are encouraged to step into the wonderment of art experiences.

Before exploring these exciting experiences which are fundamental to art and to growing, we must first clarify our own thinking. What are we seeking? Basically, we are trying to lead children into experiences which will involve them in: *touching, seeing, tasting, hearing,* and *smelling* the things in their world; and we also want them to become involved in experiences which lead to: *imagining, exploring, reasoning, inventing, experimenting, investigating,* and *selecting,* so that these experiences will be not only rich in themselves but lead to personal creative growth.

Basic to this book is the underlying premise that early stimulation of the child's *sensory* mechanisms is essential to free his creative power. In the words of Viktor Lowenfeld,[2] a great art educator:

We cannot start early enough in life. There are no limitations. Expose the baby to the lulling noise of a brook; make him conscious of it by saying, 'listen.' Let him listen to the singing of a bird, the hushing of the wind through the trees. Make him aware of the brittle sounds of the fall foliage under your feet. Let him hold and touch whatever the opportunity offers. Open his eyes to whatever you are able to take in. One of my most precious memories is the moment in my childhood when I walked with my mother through the fields and saw the miracles of nature she made me see. Whatever you can do to encourage your child in his sensitive use of his eyes, ears, fingers and entire body will increase his reservoir of experience and thus help him in his art.

It therefore is the responsibility of both parent and teacher to provide the child with opportunities which will increase his understanding of the natural and man-made world. In our hands rest the means to make the child's vision flow with wonder, to quicken his imagination, and to awaken him to the joys of living. We have the opportunity to let him discover the softness of furry kittens, the scent of freshly cut lumber, the echo of a train in the night, glistening raindrops on a petal, cool mist against his cheek. In a sense, we want him to capture the full flavor of life. Awakening children to experiences of this sort is normal and precious to all human beings. Such aesthetic feelings must be cultivated deeply, for they govern the inner harmony which is so vital to the fundamental structuring of a keen mind. We must always remember that the child's mind needs to be stretched and his eyes opened to all he can perceive.

Finally, this book is for all who desire to enrich their own awareness and sensitivity to art. We must be courageous enough to take this plunge into what may at first seem foreign to our present thinking and behavior. Unless we have confidence in our own desire to explore and investigate the world, we will be hesitant in stretching the frontiers of our children's imaginations. As we engage in these experiences with children, we will take pleasure in seeing the awakening of new vistas in ourselves.

The photographs contained in the body of the text relate to the general theme of the book, although one may not necessarily find a direct reference to the text. The pictures are intended to enhance the main theme in a visually communicable form.

[2]Lowenfeld, Viktor. *Your Child and His Art,* New York: The Macmillan Company, 1960, page 26.

Contents

The landscape is filled with infinite glimpses, each transitory, each displaced by another, and another. A seed floats on the air. A fringe of mist creeps and rises from a pine-spiked ridge. A rock looks about, shoulder-deep in the snow. An apple tree scratches at a December sky. A weed, dead-brown, tangles with twig and blown leaf in a wind-trodden patch. A quarry wall resists the widening pit . . . a tumbling kaleidoscope of awesome, fleeting visual fragments.

Yar G. Chomicky,
from *Everyday Art*, Vol. 36,
Spring, 1958, page 11

Chapter 1

The Nature of Creative Thinking

How often have we heard a person exclaim, "Creative—why I can't even draw a straight line!" Yet, this very same individual may abound with untold creative power! Our first hurdle therefore, consists in understanding what we mean by such a term as *creativity*. Before we discuss this new world of creative thinking one essential point must be stated: It is possible to be a creative person without becoming a professional artist. It is true that artists are very creative people. However, there are also creative bricklayers, chemists, doctors, chefs, electricians, salesmen, parents and teachers! The key in understanding this point is to remember that all creative people do not deal in *special-talent* products. Your type of creativeness refers to your ideas, feelings, and experiences. For our purpose, let's begin right now by thinking of creativeness as a special way of learning, thinking, and perceiving.

Most individuals have the natural endowments necessary to become more creative persons. However, not everyone's creativeness has been stirred. In many it lies slumbering be-

1

neath the surface, waiting for the moment when it can awaken and enrich fresh, unique ways of seeing. When creative potential remains in such a passive state, it collects mental dust. The term creative *functioning* is applied to those teachers, students, and parents who seek to brush away the cobwebs of dull routines and conventional living (the villains of creative thinking).

What Do the Experts Say About Creativeness?

Before we embark on our new adventure into the ever-changing, always challenging arena of creative exploration, it is important that we first understand what the experts mean when they speak of the creative person. As a point of reference, we have carefully chosen selected personnel from the sciences and the visual arts as our group of experts. Here is what they say about creativity:

Creativity is the ability to invent new symbols and ideas, to improvise on established symbols, to rearrange established organizations into new organizations, and to integrate new or borrowed ideas into previously organized systems or situations.

JUNE KING McFEE[1]

Creativity is a process of individual experience which enhances the self. It is an expression of one's uniqueness. To be creative then is to be oneself.

MICHAEL F. ANDREWS[2]

Creativity is an instinct which all people possess, an instinct with which we were born. It is the instinct which we primarily use to solve and express life's problems . . . Creativity, the ability to explore and investigate, belongs to one of the Basic Drives, a drive without which man cannot exist.

VIKTOR LOWENFELD[3]

Creativity is action by an individual through a medium. There are many avenues in human experience for creative action, but they vary according to the potentialities and the character of the particular media they offer.

MANUEL BARKAN[4]

Creativity as interactive learning brings in life. The process becomes a matter of responsiveness to all in life that is coming in and going out, and thus refers to a continual process of rejecting and accepting, making and destroying, revising and adding, and failing and succeeding.

ROBERT C. BURKHART[5]

We are concerned here with the development of people who think imaginatively, who have original ideas and welcome opportunities to put them into action.

F. LOUIS HOOVER[6]

Creativity is found in people, but not by the use of a microscope or dissecting instruments. Rather, according to the literature, it can be found in how people behave: inventing, planning, composing, constructing—behaving in such a way that others would call them creative.

W. LAMBERT BRITTAIN[7]

The creative person is both more primitive and more cultured, more destructive and more constructive, crazier and saner, than the average person.

FRANK BARRON[8]

The creative individual . . . has revealed himself . . . it is his high level of effective intelligence, his openness to experience, his esthetic sensitivity, his independence in thought and action, his high level of creative energy . . . and his unceasing striving for solutions to the ever more difficult problems that he constantly sets for himself.

DONALD W. MacKINNON[9]

Creativity requires freedom—freedom to rebel against stifling conditions, freedom to make decisions differing from those made yesterday and differing from those made by others—but it is not unlimited freedom.

ALICE MIEL[10]

. . . Creative thinkers are flexible thinkers. They readily desert old ways of thinking and strike out in new directions. . . . In the area of creativity one should certainly expect to find a trait of originality.

J. P. GUILFORD[11]

My definition, then, of the creative process is that it is the emergence in action of a novel relational product, growing out of the uniqueness of the individual on the one hand, and the materials, events, people, or circumstances of his life on the other.

CARL R. ROGERS[12]

My subjects were different from the average person in another characteristic that makes creativity more likely. Self-actualizing people are relatively unfrightened by the unknown, the mysterious, the puzzling, and often are positively attracted by it.

ABRAHAM H. MASLOW[13]

Creative learners learn by questioning, inquiring, searching, manipulating, experimenting, even playing around, but always trying to find out the truth.

E. PAUL TORRANCE[14]

Where there is faith that there will be an emergent intuition of wholeness concerning a real and internalized problem, accompanied by a readiness for commitment to its pursuit, we may speak cautiously of "creativeness." It is said to involve an open perception of self and the world and of their interaction for the sake of that which is to come. As such, it suffers the joy, despair, and dictates of a continuous, unpredictable, and irreversible dialogue with the future, for which nothing is either necessary or irrelevant. 'Up' may be 'down,' 'in' may be 'out,' 'old' may be 'new,' but the form left behind will emanate vitality, rightness, and conviction, even though it all might have been otherwise. The courage and faith to act this way I call 'creativeness,' no matter where or when or in whom it may be found.

KENNETH R. BEITTEL[15]

Creativity is a quality of uniqueness, originality, newness, or freshness which an individual voluntarily, perhaps intuitively, contributes to the conception and development of an idea.

Creativity, in my sense of its meaning, must be affected by, though it is not identical with, aesthetics. Probably because the two main ingredients of the arts are uniqueness (or creativity) and superbly high quality (or aesthetics), I see creativity as one of two fundamentally inseparable elements of the arts, and

I frankly cannot see it used as a synonym for new ways of advertising products, managing personnel, building scientific devices, mailing letters, or sailing a boat.

HOWARD CONANT[16]

What Are Creative People Like?

Our experts have provided us with a composite picture. Let's slow this action down and see what traits are unique to creative people. Creative people seem to have many characteristics in common. Here are some of them:

1. Creative people are extremely alert perceptually. That is,
   They are observant of the world about them.
   They are aware of the way things feel to the touch.
   They listen to the sounds of life around them.
   They have a sensitivity for the way things smell.
   They are aware of the taste of things.

2. Creative people are builders of their ideas. That is,
   They like to construct things in materials.
   They prefer to rearrange old ideas into new relationships.
   They like to experiment with various approaches and media.
   They like to try out new methods and techniques.
   They prefer to manipulate their ideas in various ways.
   They like to solve problems which they set for themselves.
   They seek to push the boundaries of their thinking.

3. Creative people like to explore new ideas. That is,
   They are very original in their thoughts about things.
   They like to invent new ways of saying and telling.
   They like to dream about new possibilities.
   They like to imagine and pretend.

4. Creative people are confident in themselves. That is,
   They are flexible in their approaches to situations.
   They like to be independent and on their own.
   They are outwardly expressive about what they have to say.
   They are not afraid to have emotional feelings and to show them.

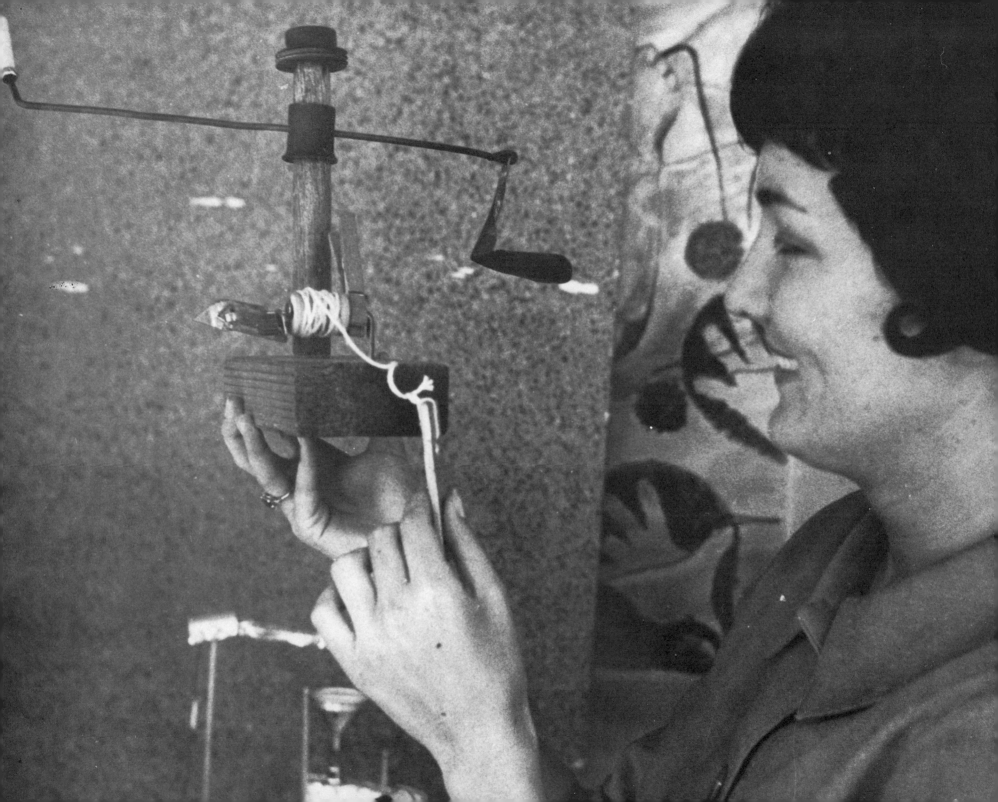

5. Creative people like to investigate the nature of things. That is,
They like to search for the meaning of things.
They question available data and information.
They like to inquire into unknown quantities.
They discover new relationships.
They desire to uncover new meanings.

6. Creative people are sensitive to aesthetic stimuli. That is,
They are sensitive to the beauty in man and nature.
They appreciate beauty that man has made.
They have a feeling for harmony and rhythm.
They like to sing, dance, and write.

These qualities, then, are intended to become the tentative goals. With this book as a guide, it will be possible for teacher, parent, or student to increase his own creative abilities. In addition, each will be able to increase the creativeness of those students or children with whom he works.

Art Experiences Are Fundamental to Art and to Creative Development

As one becomes involved with the ideas and approaches in this book, the term creative thinking is closely akin to what is meant by art experiences. This book has two general objectives. First, it intends to enrich the perceptions and thinking of the teacher, and ultimately to enrich the inventive thinking of those whom she will teach. Second, it intends to expand one's knowledge and skills in practicing art. Both of these objectives are interactive with each other. An increased understanding in one phase will modify and shape one's thinking in the other. Thus, both art development and creative thinking are interlocked.

The Aims of Art Practice and Creative Thinking

Art is a way to enrich individual awareness and understanding of the world of nature and the world of man through an increased development of the sensory mechanisms, i.e., learning to observe, feel, listen, smell, and taste.

Art is a way to develop skills in the use of art materials through experimentation, manipulation, and practice.

Art is a way to enrich appreciation of artists, art works, and aesthetic forms.

Art is a way of becoming a creative person.

Art is a way to become a flexible, confident person through telling and saying your ideas in a visual language.

Art is a way to clarify and fix ideas in the mind through visual reiteration, by strengthening what has been learned about something.

References

1. McFee, June King, *Preparation for Art*, Belmont, California: Wadsworth Publishing Company, 1961.
2. Andrews, Michael F., "The Dialectics of Creativity and Mental Health," *Creativity and Psychological Health*, Syracuse: Syracuse University Press, 1961.
3. Lowenfeld, Viktor, *Creative and Mental Growth*, New York: Macmillan Co., 1960.
4. Barkan, Manuel, *A Foundation for Art Education*, New York: The Ronald Press, 1955.
5. Burkhart, Robert C., *Spontaneous and Deliberate Ways of Learning*, Scranton: International Textbook Company, 1962.
6. Hoover, F. Louis, *Art Activities for the Very Young*, Worcester, Massachusetts: Davis Publications, Inc., 1961.
7. Brittain, W. Lambert, "Children's Art," *Cornell Extension Bulletin 1067*, Ithaca, New York: New York State College of Home Economics, August, 1961.
8. Barron, Frank, "Psychology of Imagination," *Scientific American*, 199:50, 150-156, September, 1958.
9. MacKinnon, Donald W., "What Makes a Person Creative?" pp. 15-17, *Saturday Review*, February 10, 1962.
10. Miel, Alice, et. al., *Creativity: Invitations and Instances*, Belmont, California: Wadsworth Publishing Company, 1961.

11. Guilford, J. P., *Creativity and Its Cultivation,* New York: Harper and Brothers, (edited by Harold H. Anderson), 1959.

12. Rogers, Carl R., *Creativity and Its Cultivation,* (edited by Harold H. Anderson), New York: Harper and Brothers, 1959.

13. Maslow, Abraham H., *Creativity and Its Cultivation,* (edited by Harold H. Anderson), New York: Harper and Brothers, 1959.

14. Torrance, E. Paul, Statement from an address presented at Sacramento State College, California, Spring, 1962.

15. Beittel, Kenneth R., Statement is from the context of a letter sent to the authors. Professor Beittel is Director of Research for the Department of Art Education at Pennsylvania State University, 1963.

16. Statement from an address delivered at the George Peabody College for Teachers, Nashville, Tennessee, July 9, 1963. Title of the talk was "An Artist-Educator Views Creativity and Aesthetics."

Additional Reference Sources

Anderson, Harold, editor, *Creativity and Its Cultivation,* New York: Harper and Brothers, 1959.

Barkan, Manuel, *Through Art to Creativity,* Boston: Allyn and Bacon, 1962.

Brittain, W. Lambert, "An Experiment Toward Measuring Creativity," *Research in Art Education 7th Yearbook,* National Art Education Association, 1956.

D'Amico, Victor, *Experiments In Creative Teaching,* New York: The Museum of Modern Art, 1960.

Linderman, Earl W., "How Do We Stimulate Children To Be Creative?", *California Parent-Teacher,* January, 1962.

Lowenfeld, Viktor, "Creativity and Art Education," *School Arts,* October, 1959.

Lowenfeld, Viktor, "Basic Aspects of Creative Teaching," *Creativity and Psychological Health,* Syracuse: Syracuse University Press, 1961.

Osborn, Alex F., *Applied Imagination: Principles and Procedures of Creative Thinking,* New York: Charles Scribner's Sons, 1957.

"Perceiving, Behaving, Becoming," Association for Supervision and Curriculum Development, *1962 Yearbook,* Washington, D.C., National Education Association, 1962.

Stein, Morris I., and Shirley J. Heinze, *Creativity and the Individual,* Glencoe: The Free Press, 1960.

Art is a way to enrich individual awareness and understanding of the world of nature. It also develops skills in the use of art media.

"Boy with Web" Ed Leos, Photographer

Photo, Courtesy: "Everyday Art" Magazine, The American Crayon Company.

Awareness develops when individuals have opportunities to investigate and explore the detailed nature of objects.

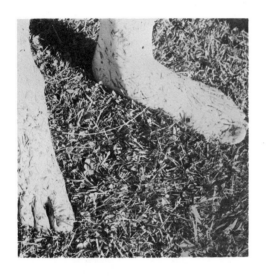

Chapter 2

Developing Readiness for Expression through Awareness

One of the most important things that a teacher or parent can help children to retain as they mature is their awareness of experiences through the use of their senses and emotions. The creative person keeps his openness to experience and in this respect he is childlike. The child does not feel that a new experience will be a risk to him. He perceives the world without feeling he has to make judgments about it. During early childhood he collects much raw material without deciding "what" or "how" he will use it. How much information is collected and what is done with it will determine his creative potential not only as a child but as an adult.

In order to have a sharper picture of how important awareness is, it would be well to understand how awareness fits into the creative procedure. The central characteristics of the creative process might well be defined as (1) awareness, (2) focus, (3) working process, and (4) art product. In this order, the first stage becomes all important to creativity of any kind.[1] Awareness entails letting the data in so that the information can be processed and stored for use. Processing and storing involves the total act of perceptual aware-

11

ness. It means taking in all sensations without immediate judging and pigeonholing of information. The second stage in the creative process is that of refining the data absorbed, in other words *focusing*. Here we begin to structure, to make form out of the formless. We relate the new data to our existing information until we have a clearer idea. Then we attempt to create or work out our focus to produce the art product.

The stages of the creative process can more readily be viewed and understood from the following explanations of the stages:

AWARENESS

1. Learning to take in information without prejudging it.
2. Being uninhibited and more free inwardly to receive information.
3. Delaying structure.
4. Trying to deliberately take in more information than usual.
5. Continuing to question a situation, observation, or judgment.
6. Getting oneself into the mood, warming up, getting into the spirit of the situation.
7. Learning to look at things from more than one point of view.

FOCUS

1. Occurs when we begin to narrow the field of data.
2. Imposes a form on things.
3. Searches over the information perceived.
4. Relates ideas, facts, sense impressions, feeling, and moods.
5. Uses the imagination to break barriers and seek new relationships.
6. Orders our experiences.
7. Keeps ideas fluid.
8. Begins to structure bits of information.

9. Begins to put the data into an order. If it doesn't fit, go to awareness again. Awareness and focus are interrelated.

WORKING PROCESS

1. Refers to production, the activity, or creative process.
2. Refers to intense and total involvement.
3. Refers to the skill of the person.
4. Refers to ordering, working hard, forming, being responsible.

ART PRODUCT

1. Refers to the finished product.
2. Refers to the feeling of being finished for the moment.
3. Refers to the culmination of the previous stages.
4. Refers to making the final judgment to stop.
5. Refers to the expression of the person as seen in the product. *Openness starts again.*

Breaking Barriers To Awareness

In order to be able to assist the child to develop awareness we must be more open to our *own* experiences. We must develop our *own* sensitivity, our *own* awareness. One effective method is to start with those children's books which are written with a high degree of sensitivity. Many of these offer unique avenues of exploration. Such an example of enriching the concept for one specific detail is dealt with in a book called *A Tail Is a Tail*, by Katherine Mace.[2] This little book tells all about animal tails and what some of them are used for.

Many approaches that we use to develop awareness are indirect and are not a conscious dissecting. They involve aesthetic experiences by exposure. Openness is referred to as the exposure stage by some psychologists. They explain that during this

Knowledge stems from a point of view. A tree is made of many visually and tactually perceived details. What details can we remember about trees? How many ways can we think of to increase our awareness? How have these pictures modified our concept of a tree?

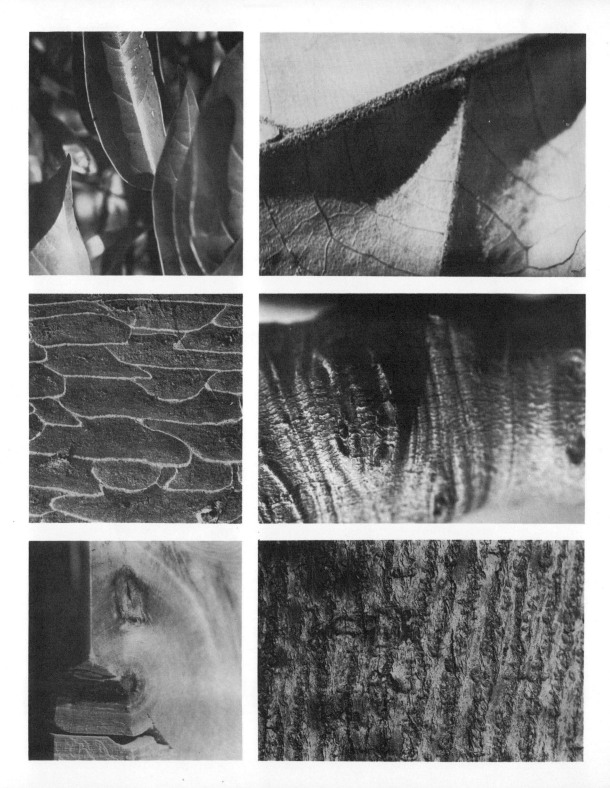

The point of observation changes the meaning of an object and may bring out details previously missed. Looking UP and looking D O W N, as well as looking straight ahead can i n c r e a s e awareness.

period the individual takes in or absorbs raw material for later use in creative expression. It is important to lead the child into experiences but to let him discover things for himself. He must perceive his environment in his own way. He should not be told how a thing smells. Rather, encourage him to explain what the smell is like or what it means to him. Experiences such as these should involve ordinary things that occur daily. Awareness requires daily practice. Don't hurry the child to answer because this forces him to a premature focus. Encourage him to perceive but not to judge; to enjoy the entire aesthetic experience of a flower rather than just naming its parts.

For the person who has become "dulled" to the world, an unusual or "odd-ball" approach is needed to reawaken his sensibilities. In order to penetrate into the details he must again become an observer investigating the detailed visual relationships which form the total impression. As Lowenfeld states, "Unless we penetrate into an experience, whatever its nature may be, it will remain superficial and as such cannot serve as the basis for creativity."[3]

Awareness Means to Eliminate the Risk to the Inner Self

Probably one of the most important points to remember when considering whether we have what it takes to be more creative persons is to remember that we are competing only with ourselves. We tend to set up our own set of stumbling blocks. To avoid taking a risk, we may use such devices as stating, "I can't do that," "I don't know how to draw a straight line," "I have never done that before," "I can't think of anything to paint," or "I don't know what to do." These all are ways we have of protecting ourselves from a threat, the threat of doing something we haven't tried before.

So that we can better compare a person who has more perceptual openness to one who maintains a more conventional attitude toward openness let us look at the following characteristics that are somewhat typical of the two types:

THE TEACHER WHO HAS ABOVE AVERAGE AWARENESS IS MORE:	THE TEACHER WHO HAS AVERAGE OR BELOW AVERAGE AWARENESS IS MORE:
expressive in his personality and encourages this in his students.	dependent on previous routines that have been established as "practical."
open to vast quantities of raw materials in his environment.	likely to rely on set routines and patterns.
flexible and fluent in ideas and adaptable to new situations.	highly dependent on "how-to-do it" routines that give a predetermined result.
interested in searching, exploring, and experimenting with materials.	inclined to reject all new ideas as threatening to the status quo; keeps his mind closed to new or unusual approaches.
free and unthreatened by mysterious and unknown situations that arise, and is rather excited and attracted by such possibilities.	likely to travel the well trodden paths and close his eyes once general recognition is made.
humorous in his approaches.	likely to have no time for humor or play, stick to tried and true methods.
inclined to try new methods of enriching learning.	inflexible, conforming, has only solutions or ideas he used in previous situations.
likely to encourage and stress independence in thought and action that leads to individual initiative and decision.	

Awareness is what Herbert Read[4] refers to as the refined use of the senses. A second meaning refers to the ability to have a high degree of awareness with the experience undergone. Third, emphasis is placed on having more empathy with a given object.

A person who has awareness perceives more of the "raw" data from his environment through his senses, experiences, and his capacity for empathy. He reaches total awareness when he is receptive to his feeling and experiences so that he can take in new information and see things in new relationships.

Awareness to objects through refined use of our senses thus means that we discipline ourselves in such a manner that much more *detail* than usual can be perceived. To be aware, one should cultivate the discipline or habit of unstructured perceptual awareness to objects in the environment.

An eighteen-month old child is very open to his environment through his senses in that he does not have barriers, does not feel threatened, does not immediately judge the material he takes in, does not relate it, does not structure, nor does he focus or make closure on what he perceives. We might compare our own way of using our senses to the open manner in which a young child perceived a new object. When given two empty tin cans to play with, he grasped them by the open ends in each hand. As he did so, he brought them near his face and noticed the shiny insides of the cans. He then tried to place one can inside the other by holding one under his arm and putting the other can inside the one he was holding. This didn't work so he then placed one on the floor and placed the other on top of it. This worked, and one can stood on top of the other. He then tried to pick them up but did not succeed and knocked them over. He tried several times to restack them and then picked them up two at a time, but didn't succeed. He then picked up one of the cans and shouted into it and seemed to enjoy the echo of the sound. Later he put the can into his mouth and tried to bite it. At the same time he tasted it and repeated his action several times. He then dropped the can and watched it roll. Then he got up and kicked it to make it roll some more. After picking up one of the cans, he dropped an object into it and listened to the noise it made.

In this experience, the child used many of his senses to experience the tin can. He found it made a noise when he dropped it, his voice sounded different when he shouted into it. He tasted it, touched it with his tongue, found that it was hard when he bit it and that it was cold. He kicked it. He noticed the surface reflected his image. He discovered many things about an object because he was free to explore it and did not approach it already focused or with a set pattern in mind.

Another example of how "closed" adults sometimes are to the use of the sense impressions is indicated in a quote from *Vision* magazine.[5]

Helen Keller tells of a friend of hers who walked through the woods. When she was asked what she saw on her walk she replied, 'Nothing in particular.' Miss Keller could not imagine how anyone could possibly walk through the woods and see 'nothing in particular.' Helen Keller must 'see' through her fingers, because she lost her eyesight through severe illness when she was a very small child. Yet Miss Keller can appreciate the symmetry, texture, and variety of the leaves. She thrills at the touch of the smooth bark of the birch tree and the tough bark of the elm tree. She delights at the feel of the first buds on the branches and the special fragrance that announces that it is springtime.

Developing Awareness Through Experiencing Details

Another way that might help us obtain a better understanding of awareness would be to remember our personal experiences with an ordinary object such as a flower. Check under the 'yes' or 'no' column if you have ever thought about:

Detail Check Chart

	Yes	No
the weight of the flower		
how soft or hard the petals are		
how long the petals are		
how easily the petals break or fall off		

how easily the petals bend ....|..........|..........

the amount of moisture in the flower ....|..........|..........

how fragile and hollow the stem is ....|..........|..........

where the stamen is ....|..........|..........

where the nectar is ....|..........|..........

the hair follicles growing on the petals ....|..........|..........

whether or not the petals have veins ....|..........|..........

whether the stem breaks easily ....|..........|..........

the shape of the petals ....|..........|..........

what it feels like to rub the petals on your cheek ...|..........|..........

how the flower might taste ....|..........|..........

how it smells ....|..........|..........

how the color in the petals changes or blends .....|..........|..........

If you checked 'yes' on more than half, you are above average.

If you have more 'noes' than 'yeses,' you need more practice!

The key to richer awareness lies in the development of our *sensory* equipment. We must learn to investigate, explore, search, and experiment. Nothing in our environment is too small or unimportant to overlook.

Awareness to one's experience means first of all the ability to perceive and second, the ability to recall in vivid detail the thoughts, perceptions, and feelings derived from an experience. This ability to form a harmonious relationship is undoubtedly more difficult for the average adult to accomplish than simply being open to his own sensory impressions.

In relating his experiences the adult faces a greater threat to his inner self and therefore is very likely to react by saying he can't do something he is requested to do, thus eliminating the threat. Part of this attitude undoubtedly stems from the fact that since early childhood we are told not to have feelings and later as an adult we are told to hide our feelings. We are told not to cry when we are injured (It didn't hurt, did it!) until we become so protective of ourselves that we can no longer identify with our emotions.

In speaking of a child's emotional reactions we mean how he felt when he was lost in a big store; how excited he was when he took a train ride; how sad he felt when his canary died; how happy he was at his birthday party; how he enjoyed sharing popcorn with a friend; how he loves to have Daddy read to him at bedtime; how sorry he felt when he hurt a playmate; and how angry he was when an older child took his tricycle away from him. His "feeling" might sometimes be more physical in nature and deal with such common experiences as a stomach-ache, or falling and hurting his knee. These are all experiences he has gone through, been a part of, participated in. He will also have sensory perceptions to relate to the emotional experiences when asked to express his reaction through art materials.

Developing Awareness Through Experiences

In order to help you identify with the meaning of awareness to one's experiences, read the questions on the chart following. We will use experiences with flowers again in order to clarify the three areas of openness being considered. Check under 'yes' or 'no' if you have ever:

Experience Check Chart

	Yes	No
planted flower seeds and watched them grow		
bought a bouquet of flowers		
picked or cut flowers		
given someone a present of flowers on some special occasion		
smelled flowers in relation to funerals, weddings, state fairs, etc.		
held or carried flowers on May Day, for a wedding or for your mother as she cut them		
worn a flower for a special occasion		
arranged flowers for the table		
visited a florist shop, flower garden		
destroyed a flower to see how it is put together		

If more 'yeses' than 'noes' were checked you have had enough experiences to select one to recall in greater detail. You have experienced "flowers" in many ways. Let's take the first point on the list and ask ourselves some questions to deepen and broaden our understanding of an experience. When you planted the flower seeds, did you notice the size, shape, weight, and color? Was the ground sun-warmed and moist? Did you crumble the dirt in your hands and smell it? Were your knees tired from kneeling on the ground? Did you uncover worms as you dug? Did you make straight rows for the seeds? Did you mark the spot where you planted them? Did you cover them with soft earth, etc., etc.?

Developing Awareness Through Empathy or Identification

The third and final way we might consider perceptual awareness is through empathy or identification with the object in the sense that we become the object. We might use the example of the flower again. In checking the following, you should begin not only to gain an understanding of empathy but also to increase your understanding of it by stretching your own barriers a little. Have you ever thought how it feels:

Empathy Check Chart

	Yes	No
to have the sun warm you		
to open in the morning and close at night		
to fall off the bush		
to feel the dew collect on you at night		
to have a bee take nectar from you		
to wave in the wind and bump into other flowers		
to get cold at night		
to turn and face the sun		
to be pulled, picked, or cut off		
to have someone put his nose in your face and sniff		

to have bugs crawl over you, maybe even eat you		
to feel the rain beat on you during a thunderstorm		
to be a flower of many colors		
to open from a tiny bud to a full blossom		
to change from the flower to the seed		

If more of these were checked 'yes' than 'no' you are well on your way to creative thinking. If you answered more 'noes,' you need more practice to develop your skill in closer identification.

A Tail Is a Tail[2] by Katherine Mace is a book that demonstrates not only fluency about tails but helps one identify with an animal that has a tail. By the time we finish reading this book to a child, we are likely to look behind us to see if we have a tail; that is, if we have identified to a high degree with the material presented.

Of Course You Are A Horse[6] by Abner Graboff is another child's book that could start one on the road to increased identification. The emphasis in this book is on pretending or imagining that we are something and then acting it out. There are many other books, records, pictures and films that can help us to develop perceptual openness and empathy.

To help a child develop perceptual openness we should always refer to other aspects rather than merely learning the name of the object. Machines can be programmed to reiterate a whole category of names, but machines have never looked at an object, smelled it, listened to it, touched it, or had any feelings about it. Your questions should be directed at the differences and similarities; to the shape as well as color.

Hailstones and Halibut Bones[7] by Mary O'Neill is an excellent book for a teacher to read to a young child on the perception of color. *Do You Hear What I Hear?*[8] by Helen Borten is a book

Increased awareness of height and
size can be experienced in many ways.
We can experience perceptive qualities through other parts of our body,
such as hands and knees, as well as
our eyes. In this way, basic information vital to art expression develops.

Enlarging or magnifying parts reveals new meanings about common objects we have viewed many times before, and missed.

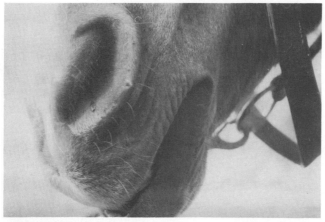

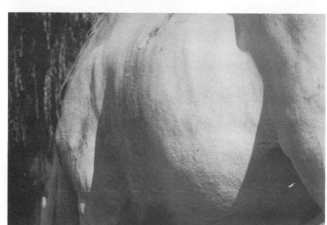
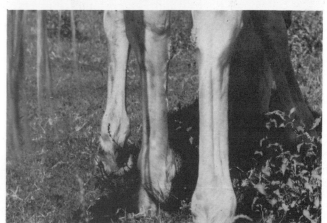

How many ways can a horse be experienced?

How does it feel when riding a horse?

What is the nose like?

Do horses have ribs?

How would it feel to bite off some grass?

How tall is a horse?

What do horses' legs look like?

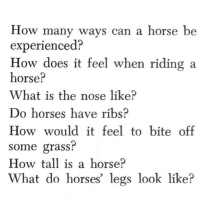
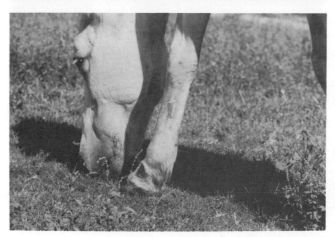

that deals with sounds from those beyond human range, such as a daisy-petal's fall, to the sound of a full symphony orchestra. When a child hears something ask him if it is loud, soft, muffled, rhythmic, or hesitant. Can he relate this to some other perception of sound? In answering such questions he will learn to discriminate differences, subtle similarities, and relate them to other sense impressions.

This is training for a more creative attitude since highly creative people (see McFee, Eisner, Guilford, Kelley, Torrance, Barron and Rogers) not only respond in unique ways to their experiences but also observe in greater detail and take in much more of the unique aspects of their environment. They also see more differences and similarities than the average person and bring more facts to bear on one aspect of a problem because they have perceived more through their senses.

Do You See What I See?[9] by Helen Borten is another example of the type of book adults could use for themselves or read to children to rediscover the sense of sight. It talks about the variety of shapes, lines, and colors that surround us. *The Wing of a Flea*[10] is a book about shapes by Ed Emberley that points out shapes in our environment that we keep missing when we look at the world with dulled eyes. These books (see additional reference sources at end of chapter for a more extensive list) deal not only with the pure perception of sounds, shapes, colors, and lines but also with the feelings they evoke in us.

It should be emphasized that all three aspects of perceptual awareness will be brought into play whenever the adult or child engages in the creative process. It is only when he brings all three into an aesthetic relationship that he achieves a momentary wholeness. As Herbert Read has stated of art, "no other subject is capable of giving the child a consciousness in which image and concept, sensation and thought, are correlated and unified . . ."[4]

In summary, our awareness goals should be:

1. To try to be more open when faced with a situation involving sensory perceptions. Don't try to structure it before perceiving it!

2. To try to find new ways to "take in" something; an unusual view, whether through sound, sight or other senses.

3. To try to remember some of the delightful as well as the painful perceptual experiences of childhood and proceed in like manner to re-experience the world.

4. To try to identify with the experiences of others.

References

1. Foshay, Arthur, "The Creative Process Described," in Creativity in Teaching ed. by Alice Miel, Belmont, California: Wadsworth Publishing Co., 1961.
2. Mace, Katherine, *A Tail Is a Tail,* New York: Abelard-Schuman, 1960.
3. Lowenfeld, Viktor, "Basic Aspects of Creative Teaching," *Creativity and Psychological Health,* edited by Michael F. Andrews, Syracuse, New York: Syracuse University Press, 1961.
4. Read, Herbert, *Education Through Art,* London: Faber and Faber, Ltd., 1944.
5. Syverson, Arthur, "Seeing Things," *Vision,* March 12, 1961, Vol. 54, No. 11.
6. Graboff, Abner, *Of Course You Are a Horse,* New York: Abelard-Schuman, 1961.
7. O'Neill, Mary, *Hailstones and Halibut Bones,* Garden City, New York: Doubleday and Co., 1961.
8. Borten, Helen, *Do You Hear What I Hear?,* New York: Abelard-Schuman, 1960.
9. Borten, Helen, *Do You See What I See?,* New York: Abelard-Schuman, 1961.
10. Emberley, Ed , *The Wing of a Flea,* Boston: Little Brown and Co., 1960.

Additional Reference Sources

Eisner, Elliot,"Children's Creativity in Art," *Studies in Art Education,* Spring, 1963.

When we imagine, we extend our vision and increase our openness. Where do the insects live? Are there craters on the moon? Do the gears move? Is there a parking lot? What else can you see?

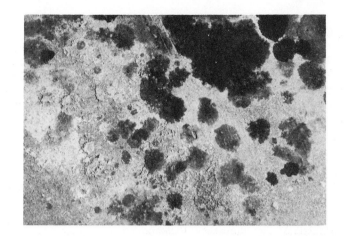

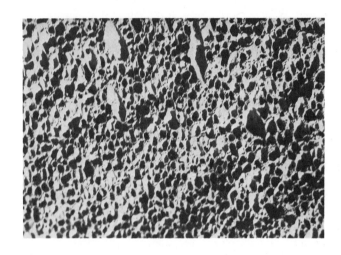

"How to Encourage Creativity in Children," *Good Housekeeping*, August, 1962, pp. 136-7.

Linderman, Earl W., "A Magic Touch," *Arts and Activities*, May, 1962.

Linderman, Earl W., "A Thing of Beauty," *Grade Teacher*, April, 1963.

Linderman, Earl W., "What is a Good Teacher?" *Arts and Activities*, October, 1963.

Linderman, Earl W., "Developing Perceptual Awareness," *Arts and Activities*, December, 1962.

Linderman, Earl W., "Let's Learn About Art," *Arts and Activities*, December, 1963.

Platt, John R., "The Fifth Need Of Man," *Horizon*, July, 1959, Vol. 1, No. 6.

Rannells, Edward, "Experience and Expression," *Art Education Bulletin*, November, 1961, Vol. 18, No. 8, pp. 14-18.

Taylor, Irving, "The Nature of The Creative Process," in *Creativity—An Examination of the Creative Process*, ed. Paul Smith, New York: Hastings House Publishers, Inc., 1959.

Von Bargen, Dora, "Motivating Young Children," *Arts and Activities*, February, 1962, Vol. 5, No. 1.

Books to Help Children Become Sensitized to One Subject, Exploring It From Many Viewpoints

Bartlett, Margaret, *Where the Brook Begins*, New York: Crowell, 1959.

Conklin, Gladys, *I Like Caterpillars*, New York: Holiday House, 1958.

Conklin, Gladys, *I Like Butterflies*, New York: Holiday House, 1960.

de Regniers, Beatrice Schenk, *The Shadow Book*, New York: Harcourt Brace, 1960.

Gordon, Isabel, *The ABC Hunt*, New York: Viking Press, 1961.

Hay, John, and Arlene Strong, *A Sense of Nature*, New York: Doubleday, 1962.

Huntington, Harriet, *Let's Go Outdoors*, New York: Doubleday, 1939.

Mace, Katherine, *A Tail Is a Tail*, New York: Abelard-Schuman, 1960.

McGrath, Thomas, *The Beautiful Things*, New York: Vanguard Press, Inc., 1960.

Mathewson, Robert, *The How and Why Wonder Book of Birds*, New York: Wonder Books, 1960.

Montresor, Beni, *House of Flowers, House of Stars*, New York: Alfred A. Knopf, 1962.

Paschel, Herbert, *The First Book of Color*, New York: F. Watts, 1959.

Rood, Ronald N., *The How and Why Wonder Book of Insects*, New York: Wonder Books, 1960.

Shuttelsworth, Dorothy, *The Story of Spiders*, Garden City, New York: Doubleday, 1959.

Udry, Janice May, *A Tree Is Nice*, New York: Harper and Brothers, 1956.

Williamson, Margaret, *The First Book of Bugs*, New York: F. Watts, 1949.

Zim, Herbert, *Goldfish*, New York: Wm. Morrow and Co., 1947.

Books to Help Children Sharpen Their Senses of Seeing, Smelling, Hearing, Touching, Tasting

Borten, Helen, *Do You Hear What I Hear?*, New York: Abelard-Schuman, 1960.

Borten, Helen, *Do You See What I See?*, New York: Abelard-Schuman, 1961.

Elkin, Benjamin, *The Loudest Noise in the World*, New York: Viking Press, 1954.

Emberley, Ed, *The Wing of a Flea*, Boston: Little, Brown & Co., 1960.

Fisher, Aileen, *Going Barefoot*, New York: Thomas Y. Crowell, 1960.

McGrath, Thomas, *The Beautiful Things*, New York: Vanguard, 1960.

Marks, Marcia, *Swing Me, Swing Tree*, Boston: Little, Brown and Co., 1959.

O'Neill, Mary, *Hailstones and Halibut Bones*, Garden City, New York: Doubleday, 1961.

Schwartz, J., *Through the Magnifying Glass*, New York: Whittlesey House, 1954.

Showers, Paul, *The Listening Walk*, New York; Thomas Y. Crowell, Co., 1961.

Showers, Paul, *Find Out by Touching*, New York: Thomas Y. Crowell, 1961.

Spooner, Jane, *Tony Plays with Sounds*, New York: John Day Co., 1961.

Webber, Irma E., *It Looks Like This*, New York: William R. Scott, Inc., 1958.

Books to Help Children Respond and Identify Emotionally With Other People, Objects, or Situations

Brown, Margaret Wise, *The House of a Hundred Windows*, New York: Harper & Brothers, 1945.

Brown, Margaret Wise, *The Dead Bird*, New York: Young Scott Brooks, 1958.

Buckley, Peter, *Jan of Holland*, New York: Watts, 1956.

Ciardi, John, *I Met a Man*, Boston: Houghton Mifflin, 1961.

Conger, Marion, *Who Has Seen the Wind?*, New York: Abingdon Press, 1959.

Crowell, Pers, *What Can a Horse Do That You Can't Do?* New York: Whittlesey House, 1954.

de Regniers, Beatrice, and Haas, Ire,*Something Special*, New York: Harcourt Brace and Co., 1958.

Fenton, Edward, *Fierce John*, Garden City, New York: Doubleday, 1959.

Frost, Robert, *You Come Too*, New York: Henry Holt, 1959.

Graboff, Abner, *Of Course, You're a Horse*, New York: Abelard-Schuman, 1959.

Huntington, Harriet, *Let's Go Outdoors*, New York: Doubleday & Co., 1939.

Icenhower, J. B., *Antarctic*, New York: Watts, 1956.

Ilionni, Leo, *Little Blue and Little Yellow*, New York: McDowell, Obolensky, 1959.

Keats, Ezra J., *The Snowy Day*, New York: Viking Press, 1962.

Lenski, Lois, *Now It's Fall*, New York: Oxford University Press, 1948.

Livingston, Myra Cohn, *Whispers and Other Poems*, New York: Harcourt Brace and Co., 1960.

Rounds, Glen, *Wildlife at Your Doorstep*, Englewood Cliffs, New Jersey: Prentice-Hall, Inc., 1958.

Schulz, Charlie, *Happiness Is a Warm Puppy*, San Francisco: Determined Productions, 1962.

Schulz, Charlie, *Security Is a Thumb and a Blanket*, San Francisco: Determined Productions, 1963.

Tressel, Alvin, *White Snow, Bright Snow*, New York: Lothrop, Lee and Shepard, 1947.

Stages of scribbling.

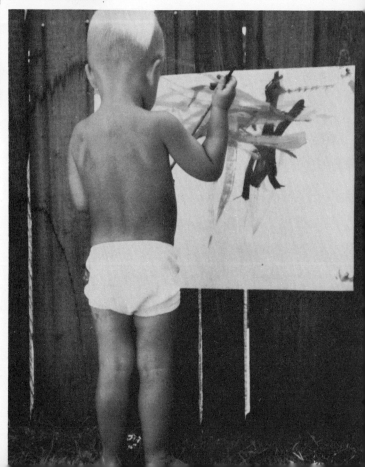

Children may be likened to a handful of seeds from many flowers. At first they may seem more similar than different in many respects. Place these seeds in the earth and nourish them. As they grow and mature their differences become marked. Some remain small and delicate while others are large and brilliant, some bloom early and some late. One thing they may have in common: under good conditions, they all bloom and have their own beauty.

Edward L. Mattil,
from *Meaning in Crafts,*
Englewood Cliffs, New Jersey: Prentice-Hall,
1959, page 3.

Chapter 3

Child Art Development and Evaluation

Scribbling: The First Stage of Art Development

Don't tell a soul but Leonardo Da Vinci was once a scribbler! Hard to believe? But alas! Each of us once scribbled! Fascinating as it may seem, the beginning of all artistic expression has its origin in the earliest scribblings of childhood. Let's tip the hourglass topsy-turvy for a moment, and return to that magical, sugar-coated land of our early years.

How does art begin? At the very start the child begins by making indistinguishable marks on a table, wall, or paper. He uses any available instrument—crayon, pencil, chalk, or even a spoonful of applesauce. The two- or three-year-old has little muscular control over his scribbling actions. He is simply delighted to discover the lines he is able to make on a particular surface. In these early beginnings he is only aware of the discovery of a newly found ability. If the child has an opportunity to *practice* his scribbling, he will soon develop more control and learn to guide the direction of his lines.

Generally speaking, children scribble between the ages of two and four. Children are in the beginning stages of art if they scribble in an uncontrolled fashion. When the child

From scribbles come these earliest symbols for man.

The child explores and finds his way beyond the symbol for man, thus extending his ability to reason and invent.

As the child gains control over his art tools and materials, he continues to invent different ways of making visual symbols to tell his thoughts. In this manner, he clarifies his personal ideas through art.

has had an opportunity to practice his art, his scribbles become more controlled. After the child has practiced his scribbling for a sufficient time, he may one day begin to tell stories in connection with his drawings.

As he draws he may converse to himself, e.g.,

This is a train. Choo choo choo.

This is a house.

Here is a bird.

When the child has reached this last level of scribbling, he begins to think in terms of words and picture images. His lines may even take on the form of fragmentary figures or crude looking houses, animals and trees.

For teachers who work with children who are at the scribbling stage here is what can be done to help them in their art development:

1. Provide a work space where the child can draw his own scribbles.
2. Do *not* show him how to improve his scribbles by suggesting that he imitate adult masterpieces.
3. Do *not* interfere with his activity by asking questions or otherwise distracting him.
4. Provide the proper art materials. Here is a list of the most suitable art materials for children who are in the scribbling stages of their art development:

Proper Art Materials for Children 2 to 4 Years Old

1. Assorted colors and sizes of crayons.
2. White, manila or newsprint paper, sizes 12" x 18" or 18" x 24".
3. Kindergarten-size brushes ½" to 1" brush width.
4. Poster paint (available in powdered or liquid form).

5. Smock or apron.
6. Paint containers (cans) and sponge to wipe brush.
7. Chalk for chalkboard or sidewalk.
8. Modeling materials, salt and flour mix, playdough.

The Symbol Stage of Art Development: Ages 4 to 8

To teachers and parents, it sometimes seems as though the little child will never stop scribbling. Then one day when least expected, he begins to draw pictures which can no longer be considered scribbles. Hurray, we say! He's going to be an artist!

Wouldn't it be wonderful if life were that simple! Of course, through the uninhibited vision of children, things do take on a pure, refreshing glow. When we look at children's art works it is very important that we also open our minds to the beauty of their artistic vision.

When through practice children have developed their artistic expression to a greater degree and in accord with their age level, their former scribbles will evolve into rudimentary figures of all sorts. The first signs of such a change can be visually detected at the kindergarten level. Circular motions become heads and tree tops, while longer strokes become legs, arms, tree trunks, and ground lines.

It can be observed that figures, trees, and other objects do not actually look as they appear to our eyes. Always remember that children relate their ideas in a less complex fashion and in relation to *their* experiences. To a child, however, these first representations of reality are giant steps in his thinking!

The most typical method in which children represent their ideas about things is through the use of simple geometric forms. These forms, a direct outgrowth of the child's former scribbling strokes, become the symbols which represent his understanding of the world he experiences. The child's pictures are certainly not "correct" or in "proportion" or even "realistic" when compared with our grown-up standards! But children are not miniature adults—thus, their pictures are extremely "real" to their childlike manner of thinking. Learning about art is comparable to learning basic word formations. They have to begin with a basic alphabet and work from there. When children are provided with opportunities to practice their art, they soon learn to solidify concepts of their world. They develop confidence in their thinking and observational abilities during the later phases of this Symbol stage (roughly second and third grade). Their pictures show an increased addition of details, greater control, and a significant increase in art skills.

For teachers who work with this age group, here are some characteristics which should appear in children's pictures:

Identifying Characteristics of the Symbol Stage

1. Children always exaggerate the parts of their pictures which are most important to them.
2. Children usually draw the sky at the top.
3. Objects in the picture are usually drawn on a ground line on the lower part of the paper.
4. Figures will all tend to look somewhat alike. This indicates a conceptual understanding rather than a visual observation of the figure.
5. Children sometimes omit details of objects which they did not think about during their drawing experience.

Here are some suggestions to help children at this stage of development:

1. Stimulate the child to utilize his idea-factory by providing stories, films and challenging discussions of animals, plants, and people in action.

2. Make your own enthusiasms spill over so that he will get excited and catch the spark.
3. Lead the child in his thinking to the point where he can pursue an idea independently.
4. Encourage the child to be original and inventive and to always do his own work.
5. Don't be overly critical for "mistakes" are part of learning.

Proper Art Materials for Children 4 to 8 Years Old

The most suitable materials for this stage of art development include:

1. Powdered poster paints mixed to a creamy consistency.
2. Both large and small brushes (round, flat bristle, or sable).
3. Crayons of assorted colors and sizes.
4. Colored papers of assorted colors and sizes.
5. Clay, salt ceramic, or other modeling material.
6. Colored chalks.
7. Scrap materials for collage and material pictures.
8. Paint containers, smock, sponges, etc.
9. Newsprint, manila, white drawing paper, 12″ x 18″ to 24″ x 36″.
10. Glue, scissors, and paste.

Although the foregoing supplies are basic to a child's art development, the teacher will discover other possible materials.

The Beginning Realism Stage of Art Development: Ages 9 to 12

This stage is generally thought of as the last outpost for childish pictures and the beginning frontier for a new found "realistic" approach to drawing. Although children at this level

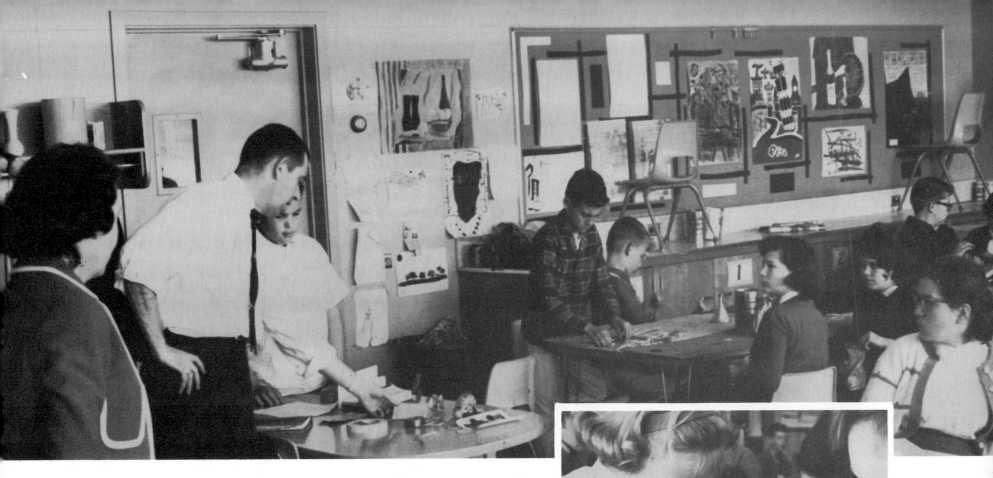

Whenever the student needs direction, the teacher guides the student towards increasing his perceptions about procedures and his skills in various art media.

The teacher instructs in procedures and thinking until the individual is deeply involved in saying what he feels is essential to a particular idea.

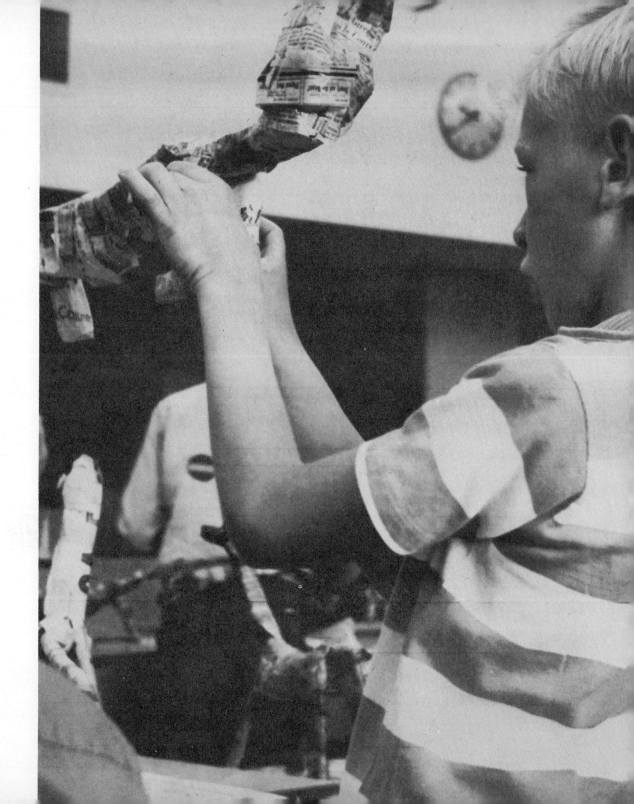

A strong motivation enables the child to imagine and relive experiences outside of himself. His ability to identify with other people, situations or things thus helps him to redefine the nature of his own creativeness.

(4th, 5th, 6th and 7th grades) still retain that uncritical blissfulness of childhood fantasy, their thinking has undergone a dramatic change. They are suddenly boy or girl, alive and bursting with a new social consciousness. The concept symbols which satisfied their earlier art works no longer suffice to represent figures, animals, or objects. The child also discovers in his drawings that the sky meets the horizon, and that objects can overlap each other, thus creating spatial effects.

In observing pictures done by children in the Beginning Realism Stage, notice that the sky touches the horizon. Observe the more "realistic" approach to the figure. Notice also the increase of details in specific objects. Figures are more in proportion with less exaggeration. Definite sex differences are apparent, such as pants or dresses. There may even be attempts to shade parts of the picture or otherwise to indicate atmospheric effects. Often there is an awareness of artistic principles such as repetition of shapes and definite spatial effects.

Identifying Characteristics of the Beginning Realism Stage

1. Children at this stage make figures which more closely resemble reality.
2. They overlap objects in their pictures to create a sense of depth.
3. They make distant objects smaller.
4. There is a definite feeling for design qualities such as repetition, color harmonies, and texturing.
5. Pictures include many more details than before.

Here are some suggestions to help children who are at this stage of their artistic development:

1. Provide the children with an opportunity to experiment, explore, and discover what materials can do.
2. Always stress skillful handling of materials.

3. Begin teaching basic art elements such as shape, line, texture, and color. Be sure to keep it at the children's level of understanding.
4. Introduce beginning concepts of perspective or ways to represent objects in space.
5. Stress the importance of personal expression of ideas in making pictures.

Proper Art Materials for Children: Ages 9 to 12

Here are materials that are most suitable for children at this stage of their art development:

Painting:
    water color paints in the tray or tube
    soft brushes of various sizes, sponge
    poster paint

Drawing:
    charcoal
    white, pastel, butcher, colored papers
    pencils
    chalks

Modeling:
    clay
    salt ceramic
    papier-mâché

Print Making:
    gadget printing, potatoes, cardboard, spools, inner tubes, etc.
    linoleum
    silk-screen

Collage:
    cloth
    papers of various sorts and sizes
    strings, yarns

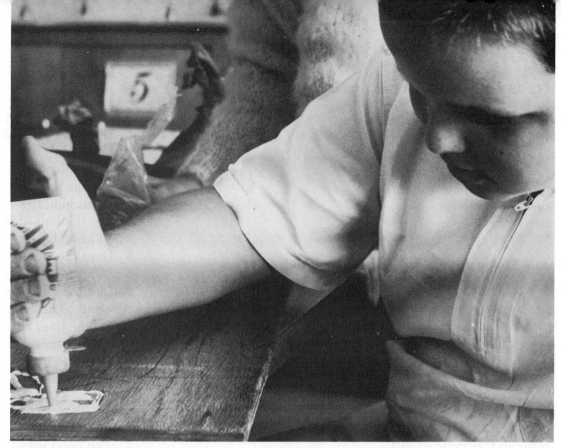

Each individual approaches new media in different ways. Some manipulate the material first while others may express ideas right from the start. Materials suggest ideas and ideas suggest materials. It is not important that one always precede the other.

Construction and Three-Dimension:
- toothpicks
- cardboard
- tagboard
- construction papers
- wires
- woods

Some Suggestions in Evaluating Children's Art

How can a teacher be certain, after providing children with a number of art experiences, that some tangible growth has taken place? Actually there are a number of definite characteristics to look for. Some of these characteristics can be found in the finished art work, in the young artists themselves.

One of the most satisfactory procedures in evaluating your art program is to collect the children's art works. Parents of a young child will be able to save all of his work. Teachers should try to save representative samples at intervals during the month. These can be returned at the close of the semester or school year. Keep each child's work in a separate folder and place the date on each picture. This will facilitate comparisons between early and later art works.

Listed following are some specific characteristics which indicate art growth. These characteristics can be used as a progress guide in evaluating children's art development.

Basic Check Points in Evaluating Children's Art Growth As Seen in Children's Pictures

A. Age: 2-4
   Grade: Preschool or Kindergarten
   Stage: *Scribbling*

Signs of Art Growth:
1. Does the child follow typical scribbling sequences as described in this chapter?
2. Does the child enjoy scribbling?
3. Are the scribbles vigorous and forceful?
   (This indicates emotional and physical growth.)
4. Are the lines distributed over the entire paper?
   (This indicates emotional and aesthetic growth.)
5. Does the child work independently?
   (This means he is more creative.)
6. Can the child control his motions?
   (This indicates muscular coordination.)
7. Do the lines change in intensity and direction?
   (This indicates flexibility.)
8. Does the child concentrate when he scribbles?
   (This indicates creative growth.)

Danger Signals:
1. The child only makes marks on the paper.
2. The child asks the teacher to draw for him.
3. The child interrupts his scribbles frequently.
4. The child tries to imitate other children and grown-ups.

B. Age: 4-8
   Grade: Kindergarten through 3rd grade
   Stage: *Symbol*
   Signs of Art Growth:
1. Does the child draw simple, geometric figures?
2. Does he exaggerate important parts?
3. Do his drawings indicate many details?
   (nostrils, eyelashes, fingers, toes, etc.)
4. Is there evidence of improvement in his images for figures, trees, houses, flowers, and animals?
5. Is the drawing distributed over the whole paper?
6. Does the child employ decoration in his work?

"Boy and Girl at Blackboard"
Ed Leos, Photographer

"Two Children at Desk"
Ed Leos, Photographer

Photo, Courtesy:
"Everyday Art" Magazine,
The American Crayon Company.

Photo, Courtesy:
"Everyday Art" Magazine,
The American Crayon Comp

"Children Watching Film"
Ed Leos, Photographer

larifies
orking

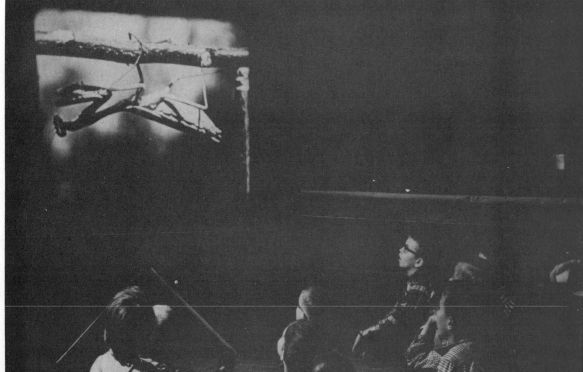

Photo, Courtesy: "Everyday Art" Magazine, The American Crayon Company.

7. Is there evidence of balance?
8. Does the child use many colors?
9. Does he use more than one value of the same color?
10. Are distant objects drawn smaller?
11. Does the child work carefully?
12. Does he finish his work?
13. Does the work indicate original ideas?
14. Is the child imaginative?
15. Does the child indicate textures by making contrasting surface treatments?

Danger Signals:

1. Does the child say "I can't"?
2. Is the drawing full of patterns and rigid stereotypes? (stick figures, v-shaped birds, etc.)
3. Does the child draw only one object such as airplanes, horses, or houses etc.?
4. Does the child make "warmed-over" pictures?
5. Is the work lacking in details and freshness?
6. Does the child like to copy?

C. Age: 9-12

Grade: 4th-7th

Stage: *Beginning Realism*

Signs of Art Growth:

1. Does the child include a horizon line in his picture?
2. Does the child include shading?
3. Do the figures look more like real people?
4. Does he include many details in his drawings?
5. Does the child make distinctions between boys and girls in his work?
6. Does the child show decorative elements in his pictures?
7. Is there a sense of balance and rhythm?
8. Is there evidence of experimentation with the medium?
9. Is the work inventive?
10. Does the child relate colors to each other?

11. Are there indications of perspective?
12. Does he overlap objects?
13. Do objects appear in proportion?

Danger Signals:

1. Do his pictures still contain geometric figures?
2. Does the child imitate others?
3. Does the child desire to copy or trace?
4. Are stick figures or patterns included in the pictures?
5. Does the child show lack of enthusiasm while he is drawing?
6. Does the child continually repeat the same subject?

Signs of Art Growth as Observed in Children's Thinking

Of course not all signs of art growth can be detected through evaluating children's pictures. Often growth is taking place, but instead of showing up immediately in their pictures, it may be evident in their thinking, attitudes, and actions. Here are some questions for detecting signs of art growth:

1. Are the children confident and eager to express ideas in art materials?
2. Do the children notice color in things around them?
3. Do they notice the way things feel to their touch?
4. Do they discuss ideas related to art?
5. Do they express more of their own ideas about things?
6. Are the children more inventive in their thinking?
7. Do they work on their art for longer periods of time?
8. Are the children more flexible in their own work?

Check Points for the Teacher

Good art teaching is most dependent on the strength of those who teach it. At the classroom level this includes both

Does the child exaggerate important parts and things?

Does the child draw simple, geometric figures?

Is the drawing distributed over the whole paper?

Is the base line or ground line included?

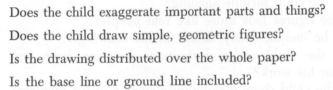

Do objects appear in proportio

Are objects overlapped?

Are there indications of persp

Do the figures look more like

Does the child include many

teachers and parents. Here are some suggestions to help those who are beginning to teach art to children:

SUGGESTED DO'S

1. Encourage the child always to do his own work.
2. Exhibit all the children's work. Don't favor the "talented ones."
3. Teach the child to be independent.
4. Encourage the children to be original and inventive.
5. Encourage the children always to finish their work.
6. Encourage the children to talk about their work.
7. Provide ample time and opportunity to engage in art.
8. Encourage children to be observant and aware.
9. Teach children to care for materials.
10. Teach children to concentrate on their thinking.
11. Encourage children to be imaginative.
12. Encourage children to experiment with materials.
13. Utilize visual aids to strengthen your teaching.
14. Always motivate with specific objectives in mind.
15. Encourage the child to think in new directions.

SUGGESTED DON'TS

1. Don't teach indoctrinary techniques which force all children to do the exact same thing.
2. Don't use pattern books, dittos, or hectographed materials.
3. Don't express fears about attempting original work.
4. Don't create the notion that art is busy work or "playtime."
5. Don't give children art materials and tell them to make "anything they would like." Very few are "self-motivated."
6. Don't use imitative methods such as copying, tracing.
7. Don't impose adult standards on the child.
8. Don't expect children always to do beautiful pictures.
9. Don't compare children's art work.
10. Don't be overly critical of children's art work. Mistakes are a necessary part of learning.
11. Don't discriminate by favoring certain children.
12. Don't use the same materials repeatedly.
13. Don't use only one size paper.
14. Don't limit art lessons to occasional fill-ins on the schedule.

Check Points on Improving Art Motivations

The most important phase of any art lesson is the art motivation. A good motivation can stimulate children's thinking and set the stage for wonderful experiences with art media. There are several points to consider in learning to present a strong motivation. Here are some suggestions when presenting art motivations to children:

1. Practice by giving art motivations to children.
2. Be dramatic! (Blanche Jefferson[1] says that when you dramatize children love it, and catch the spirit quickly.)
3. Be enthusiastic and eager to experience ideas.
4. Always start a motivation with an interesting introduction.
5. Outline objectives clearly. Know what to look for in art motivations.
6. Utilize sufficient visual material to strengthen the presentation.
7. Don't overwork the motivation by prolonging it until the children are restless. Stop at the high point.
8. Be alive and alert to each motivational situation.
9. Be sure to give the children an understanding of procedures for working with materials.

---

[1]Jefferson, Blanche. *Teaching Art to Children.* Boston: Allyn and Bacon, 2nd Ed., 1963.

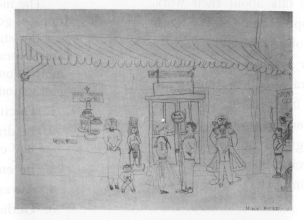

Does the child include shading?

Are there indications of realism in the picture? Does the child show decorative work in his pictures?

Is there a sense of balance and rhythm?

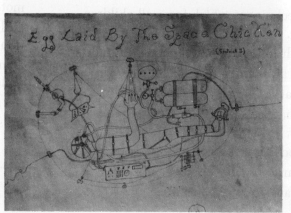

Photo, Courtesy: "Everyday Art" Magazine, The American Crayon Company.

Motivations should include many types of experiences. Texture can be felt by both sight and touch.

"Photogram of Dandelion"
Jeannine Hanson, Photographer

10. Ask questions that lead the children into discussion and search for their own ideas.

It is difficult to say how long a motivation should be. Sometimes it is brief (three to five minutes), and other times it may require a sufficient build-up (ten to twenty minutes) to stimulate the children's thinking. Usually, it is proportionate to the total length of an art lesson. Again, a general rule of thumb is to plan for approximately 30 to 60 minutes for an art lesson. Crayon work may require as little as 30 minutes for the children to finish while painting will most certainly require 60 minutes. Motivations can be as brief or as long as necessary. Some projects, such as puppets or papier mâché, may necessitate two or more periods. Trial experiences will soon help one to decide. The important thing is to *plan for specific art lessons* within the classroom program. This means that all members of the class usually should engage in such experiences at the same time. Taking a "turn" at the easel can only be supplementary to a planned program which has clearly defined objectives.

References

Alschuler, Rose H., and Hattwick, Laberta, *A Study of Painting and Personality of Young Children*, Chicago: University of Chicago Press, 1947, 2 vols.

Bland, Jane Cooper, *Art of The Young Child*, New York: Museum of Modern Art, 1960.

D'Amico, Victor, *Creative Teaching in Art*, Scranton, Pa.: International Textbook, 1942, rev. ed. 1953.

de Francesco, Italo L., *Art Education: Its Means and Ends*, New York: Harper and Brothers, 1958.

Eng, Helga, *The Psychology of Children's Drawings from the First Strokes to Coloured Drawing*, London: Paul, Trench, Truber, 1931.

Erdt, Margaret Hamilton, *Teaching Art in the Elementary School*, New York: Holt, Rinehart and Winston, rev. ed., 1962.

Gaitskell, Charles, *Children and Their Art*, New York: Harcourt, Brace and Co., 1958.

Hoover, F. Louis, *Art Activities for the Very Young*, Worcester, Mass.: Davis Publications, 1961.

Jefferson, Blanche, *Teaching Art to Children*, Boston: Allyn and Bacon, Inc., 1963. (Second Edition.)

La Tronico, Elaine, "Scylla, Charybdis, and the Art Teacher," *National Education Association Journal*, December, 1961, pp. 30-31.

Linderman, Earl, "Child Art: The Wellspring of Life," *National Catholic Kindergarten Review*, Winter-December, Vol. XIII, 1963.

Linderman, Earl, "Child Art and the Teacher," *Grade Teacher*, April 1962.

Lindstrom, Miriam, *Children's Art*, Berkeley, Calif.: University of California Press, 1957.

Lowenfeld, Viktor, *The Nature of Creative Activity*, New York: Harcourt, Brace and Co., 1939.

Lowenfeld, Viktor, *Your Child and His Art*, New York: The Macmillan Co., 1955.

Lowenfeld, Viktor, *Creative and Mental Growth*, New York: The Macmillan Company, 1960.

McFee, June King, *Preparation for Art*, Belmont, California: Wadsworth Publishing Company, 1960.

McIlvain, Dorothy S., *Art for Primary Grades*, New York: G. P. Putnam Sons, 1961.

Mendelowitz, Daniel C., *Children Are Artists*, Stanford, California: Stanford University Press, 1954.

Reshovsky, Zora, "The Wonderful World of Creative Children," *Woman's Day*, April, 1963, pp. 37-41.

"How Children Paint—Animals, People and Scenes," *The Instructor*, April, 1962.

Schaefer-Simmern, Henry, *The Unfolding of Artistic Activity*, Berkeley: University of California Press, 1948.

When we as adults take the time to observe and to study children, and to extend our own understanding of the countless ways in which young people grow and develop, the creative achievement of youth will be increased. How can we as adults stimulate this growth? We need to provide abundant creative opportunities. A child's surroundings—his world of man-made things—his world of God-made things: people, plants, animals, the sun, moon and stars—all provide infinite exploratory possibilities which will help him develop the sensitivity and the imagination so important in living. Children need to be helped to see, to feel, to listen, and to think, for out of these abilities comes the power to relate and to interpret the world around them.

Arne W. Randall and
Ruth Elise Halvorsen
from *Painting in the Classroom,*
Worcester, Massachusetts:
Davis Publications, 1962, page 5

Chapter 4

Motivation: Winding up the Mainspring of Art

"I don't know what to draw."

"I don't have any ideas."

"I can't do it."

"Show me."

How many of us have ever heard children make comments of this sort during the art lesson? What do we say to children that will stimulate in them a desire to tell their ideas and experiences with art materials? Do we simply pass out the paper and tell them to "go to work"? It is probable that a procedure of this sort would only encourage statements like those mentioned.

Before children can practice their art, they need help in practicing their thinking. We simply cannot expect most children to sit down with their art materials and pour forth a

Verbal motivations can bring about a deeper personal investigation. A richer experience leads to actualization of the self.

Firsthand experiences have direct appeal to the senses and the emotions. Art grows readily from experiences such as these.

multitude of ideas. Very young children are still fascinated by art materials and living things in general; however many school-age youngsters have already developed stop signs in their thinking. As children grow older, these stop signs may become considerably more frequent with all sorts of S-shaped curves to surpass, thus slowing down a clear view of the thinking road ahead.

If a teacher instructs a child to do a drawing or painting without providing him with any prior stimulation, there is a strong chance that he will make a generalized picture which doesn't say very much as a personal expressive statement. Pictures of this sort (which some children repeat over and over again) are the result of "warmed-over" ideas which the child has done in the past. He falls back on them when he hasn't been motivated by his experiences to say something challenging in terms of his present awareness. A typical example of the warmed-over picture is the tree-house-sun-tulip picture often seen at the primary level, and the palm tree-desert island-setting sun-ocean picture of older students. These pictures and their prototypes are frequently found hanging at the easels—the results of a "turn" at painting.

Children need direction and strong challenge in their art thinking. They need to get excited about their ideas. In order to re-create an experience through art media, the child needs to recall the experience vividly. He must be stirred sufficiently that he has a desire to communicate his thoughts in visual terms. In this respect, he needs to develop somewhat the eye of the artist. The artist is always full of ideas. He is able to select from his regenerative stockpile of thoughts the ideas most suitable to express a specific intent. In addition, he is able to tell his ideas in original and inventive ways. The artist is both a thinker and a craftsman—able to unite art skill and idea-skill into a personal technique for telling what he knows and feels about things in his world. Similarly, our objective in working with children deals

with how to stimulate *their* art thinking and develop *their* art skills in saying things with art materials. Here is where motivation comes in!

Motivation means a teacher's or parent's ability to arouse and stimulate a child's thinking so that he has a desire to communicate his ideas in visual form. It is also a way by which we can help the child to think through ideas and/or relive his experiences. Here are several different approaches to use when motivating children.

Ways to Motivate Children in Their Art

Verbal Discussions. This type of motivational procedure is used most often and is usually interactive with the other types listed. Essentially, it refers to an enlivened discussion between child and teacher. The verbal discussion should always be the basic means for challenging the child's thinking during or after he has participated in one of the following experiences.

Visual Experiences. This type of experience occurs when the teacher or parent uses films, slides, or other illustrative material to stimulate visual observation. If a film is used, the procedure might go something like this: The teacher must first select the film basing his choice on its relatively short length, its concentration of intended details, and its photographic properties. Emotional factors might also be considered. For example the film "Spider Engineers" deals with a creature somewhat repugnant to many people; thus an emotional response is quite likely. When such a film has been selected and shown, the teacher might introduce the verbal discussion with such questions as,

How would it feel to have eight legs?
How would it feel to be stuck with the spider's hypo-needle?
How would it feel to be caught in his sticky web?

The joy or frustration of self-discovery is difficult to measure from the appearance of the person. The reaction can be measured better through the growth evidenced in art processes or art products.

How would it feel to be pulled down into a dark hole and eaten?

When sufficient discussion has stimulated thinking, the children use art materials to develop their own ideas evolving from the particular film. Art materials should always be prepared ahead of time and be available for instant use at the peak of readiness. A positive factor in using films to help motivate is that they strengthen the mental image by allowing the child to focus on the details of a particular experience. Films are also invaluable in that the camera can slow down such rapid actions as birds in flight, or speed up the entire growth sequence of plants—things which the naked eye cannot witness. Thus the film enables us to see details—an important factor in artistic and creative thinking.

Firsthand Experiences. This means providing the children with actual experiences involving live animals, flowers, people, or going to various places and events. It refers to opportunities in which childen can observe, question, and investigate on-the-spot characteristics of specific things. Such experiences include going to the zoo, the farm, bringing animals to class, walking through a greenhouse, visiting a bakery, a factory, and so forth. In such activities, the teacher or parent must do more than lead the child to the object. She must encourage the child to make discoveries into the nature of the object. The teacher must lead the child along the path of inquiry to the point where *he will make the discoveries for himself*. This is done by utilizing a questioning type approach. For example, a teacher may surmise that the students need to strengthen their concepts of horses. In terms of a firsthand experience, here are some questions to lead the child into avenues of search and exploration:

Is the horse very large? How large? Is he larger than yourself?
What color is he? Is he the same color all over?
Can you see his muscles?

Does he have eyelashes? Do his eyes look like your eyes?
How does the hair grow to form his mane?
How long is his tail?
How does he bend his neck?
Who has ever ridden on a horse? Did you bounce up and down?
Can a horse run fast?
Who has ever touched a horse? What does he feel like?
Did you ever imagine that you were a horse?

Questions of this nature direct the child's thinking to specific details about horses. As the questions are asked, the child will search for visual images. In this manner, the child is able to *crystallize* his images pertaining to the experience with a horse. He should now be ready to reflect some of these images in his art expression.

Material Experiences. This refers to experimentation, search, and investigation as the child works directly in the art materials without previous stimulation. If, for instance, a child were working with clay, he would be more apt to discover possibilities and ideas by actually experimenting with it before he started to make an object. If he were experimenting with paint on a surface, the manipulation of the pigment would often suggest possibilities for investigation. In these instances it is possible for the material to be the major factor in motivating the child. The experimentation could be interspersed with questions such as:

What happens when two colors run together?
How can we make the color green?
What happens when you wet the paper first?
Let's try an ink line over our water colors.
Can you make coils with the clay?
How can you texture the surface?
What can you discover about this material?

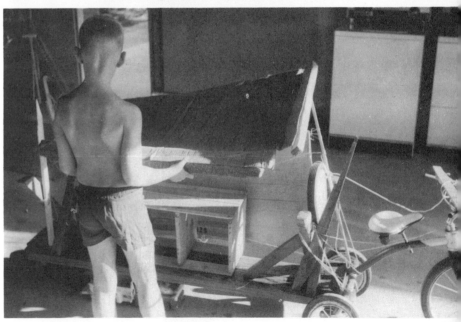

Becoming involved with materials, can be through direct contact or rather detached intellectual contemplation before creative action begins.

"Photo of Children and Skunk"
Ed Leos, Photographer
Photo, Courtesy: "Everyday Art" Magazine, The American Crayon Company.

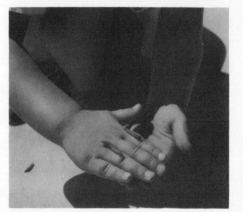

Motivations stem from a diversity of experiences. The thrill of riding, the scent of a rose, the excitement of a carnival ride, the tickle of a caterpillar, the tenderness of a hug—all combine to enrich personal aesthetic experiences.

Odd-ball or unusual materials provide a less conventional means for the adult to experiment without immediately focusing on an idea.

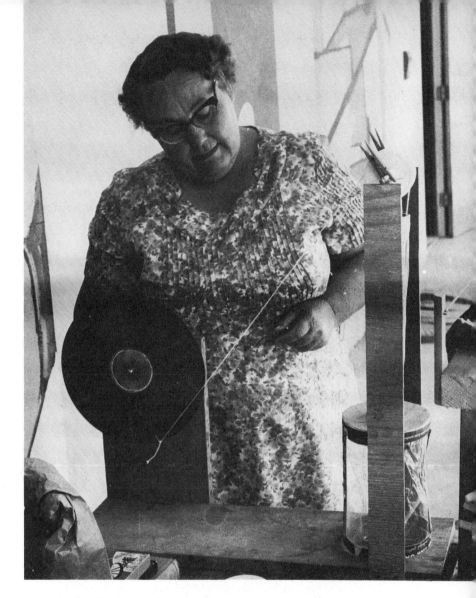

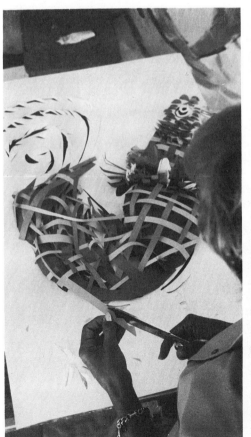

Of course all questions should be oriented to a specific grade level. At all times the teacher should guide the children and yet be ready to let *them* take the reins as soon as they can see new possibilities in the material.

Sensory Experiences. Sensory experience refers to the manner in which we perceive or "take in" outside information through the senses. We can increase our intake of information about the world around us by increasing our capacity for utilizing our senses. For our purposes this refers to visual sensitivity or learning to observe with our eyes; auditive sensitivity or learning to listen; tactile sensitivity or learning how things feel to our touch; and olfactory sensitivity or the ability to learn about things through our sense of smell. For an exercise in visual observation, the teacher could instruct each child to collect some flowers and bring them to class. The children could then examine their flowers very closely to see what they could discover. Here are some questions to ask:

What is the flower's name?

Can you count the petals? How many?

What is the shape of the petals?

Can you find the seed pockets?

What color is your flower?

Have you ever seen this color before? Where?

How tall is the stem?

How long is the stamen?

Where is the pollen located?

In a *listening experience,* the objective would be to increase our ability to listen. One method to use would be to collect as many different kinds of objects as possible, e.g., nails, hinges, glassware, dishes, twigs, sandpaper, cloth, metals, sponges, plastic objects, and whatever else is available. Next place a cardboard screen in front of the assorted objects in order to conceal their identity. Stand behind the screened objects and create various sounds by hitting, rubbing, tapping, rolling, and shaking the objects. Encourage the children to listen closely, and then attempt recognition of the sounds they hear. Again, the teacher should ask questions that will direct their thinking toward an increased awareness in responding to sounds. For example:

Can you recognize the sound?

Do you enjoy hearing these sounds?

What does this sound remind you of?

Is this a musical sound?

Which sounds are soft?

Which sounds are mellow?

Which sounds are rhythmical?

How do you feel when you hear a certain sound?

An exercise for the children would be to have them collect several objects in a box and encourage them to construct their own sound box by fastening, hanging, and positioning various materials inside of the box.

In a *tactile experience,* the objective is to encourage an awareness of differences and similarities in the "feel" of objects. The variety is endless. For example:

What is the difference between the feel of wood and stone?

Which is smoother, an egg or a glass?

What things are rough? Slippery? Soft?

Which is softer, fur or cotton? Which is warmer?

What things feel sandy? Fuzzy? Fluffy?

What things feel moist? Wet? Dry?

What things feel cool to the touch?

An exercise for tactile sensitivity would be to have the children collect differently textured objects and bring them to class. Some

Does the grass whisper?

Have you ever invented a sound machine?

possibilities include papers, spools, beans, rope, cotton, pebbles, corrugated cardboard, cloth, buttons, steel wool, and burlap. Have them also bring a lidded container, such as a shoe box. Let them construct their own "feeling-boxes" by gluing, fastening, suspending and positioning objects that have interesting textural qualities inside the boxes. After the inside is complete, have each child cut an opening in one of the sides so that the hand can reach in and explore the textures. Experiences of this nature direct the child's imagery toward tactile considerations.

In *olfactory experiences*, the objective is to increase an awareness of differences and similarities in smell. One method of stimulating this awareness is to collect various scents and put them into small bottles. Solid pieces can be crumbled with a hammer and then dropped into bottles. In this manner, an entire collection of various scents can be acquired and stored for comparison. Some possibilities for scents include pine, mint, hay, clover, sawdust, flowers, dried foods, spices, perfumes and powders. When a sufficient variety of scents has been collected, encourage the children to recognize and to develop images based on specific smells. Ask questions such as:

Which smells are pleasant?

Which smells are not pleasant?

What does the smell remind us of?

Where are such smells located?

Which one smells sweet?

Which smell is sour?

Which smell is sharp?

Which smell is mellow?

What does wet wood smell like?

Do all things have smells?

What does a rose smell like? Grass? Soil?

Does the forest have a smell?

Motivations which deal with sensory experiences are necessary for the development of a child's creative awareness. Children who are perceptually aware are more likely to inquire, explore, and express their relationships as growing, purposeful beings. In terms of their art expression they are more ably equipped to say and tell ideas which are original and inventive.

Basic Motivational Categories

For purposes of clarification, and to simplify art program planning, all art motivations can be grouped under one of the following three major classifications:

1. *Artistic motivations.*
2. *Intellectual motivations.*
3. *Imaginative motivations.*

Artistic Motivations. This refers to all art motivations which have as their aims the development of an increased sensitivity to artistic functions. Emphasis within this area should stress the *development of skills in using art media, learning to design, and becoming responsive to the beauty of natural and man-made forms.* Artistic structuring of motivations can be introduced as early as the kindergarten level, but it should be in keeping with the learning level and thinking of the child. It is never too early to begin making children aware of colors, textures, shapes, lines, and other art fundamentals. Here is a sample approach in working with children of primary school age:

(*Paints, brushes, and pertinent materials have been distributed and the children are ready to go.*) *As part of our art learning time today, who knows one of the colors in front of him? There's a hand! Good. We all know yellow . . . red . . . blue . . . What do you suppose would happen if we mixed red and yellow together? Let's try it . . . Who has discovered? Let's each of us mix two colors together and see what we can discover. We might even make something that is this color. Let's see if we can mix colors right on our paper as we paint . . .*

Tactile sensations lead to images not perceived by the eye. The individual's awareness of differences and similarities is increased through perceiving how things feel.

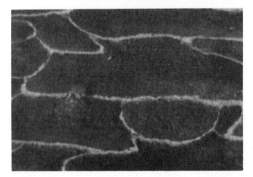

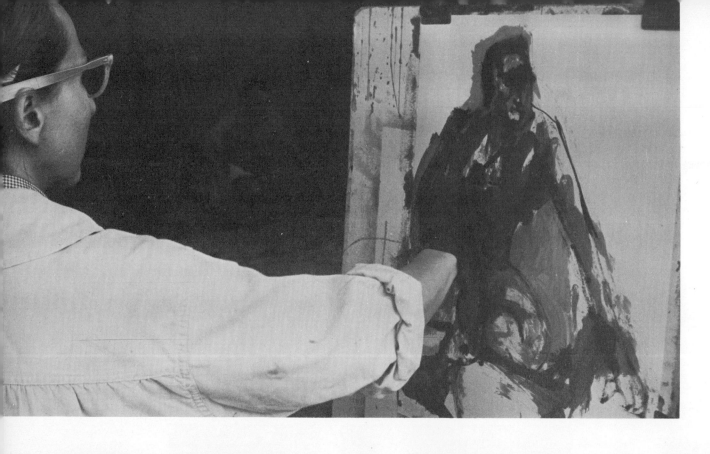

Skill and involvement of the self are essential aspects of art development.

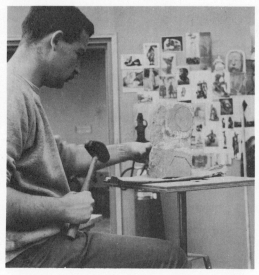

Artistic motivations do not always have to deal directly with art materials as such. Discovering beauty in natural and man-made forms can be a way to learn about artistic forms. For example, the teacher can encourage children to become more aware of beauty by leading them to observe and discover the *shape* of things. Have them collect various stones, leaves, shells, and other available objects. Point out the possible differences and similiarities in shapes. Some stones are long, some short, some lumpy, some angular, some sharply curved, and some very unusual in shape. Encourage the children to discover for themselves and to discuss what they have learned.

At the intermediate level some ideas for motivations of an *artistic nature* could include:

Experimenting with water colors	Exploring textures
Learning about perspective	Discovering colors
Learning how to design	Drawing the figure
The elements of art	Drawing landscapes
Discovering what the brush can do	Drawing trees

Here is a sample artistic motivation for drawing the figure at the intermediate grade levels:

Learning to Draw Figures

Materials. Large sheets of paper, 18″ x 24″ or larger, crayons, brushes, charcoal, pencils.

Sample Artistic Motivation. Learning to draw people means that you must be very observant and willing to practice your art skills. What are some of the ways which can help us to improve our figure drawing? Yes, using each other as models is a very good way. You could also use a large mirror if you wanted to draw yourself. When you look at others or at yourself you must look carefully to see how the head is bent, what the legs are doing,

which way the body is leaning, and all the actions that our figure is making. When we have observed carefully, we can draw what we remember about the pose we were in. When you draw figures in action, do not worry about erasing. You can make many sketching lines in your pictures, and then darken the ones which you feel are most correct. Some points to remember and look for when you are posing are:

1. Your body bends at the waist. Where else? It also bends at elbows, wrists, knees, neck and ankles.

2. Some poses to take might include bending over, stretching upward, getting ready to run, climbing a ladder. How many more can you think of?

Now we are ready to try our first pose and then to draw what we have observed and remember.

Intellectual Motivations. This refers to all art motivations that have as their aim the development and enrichment of children's concepts for natural and man-made objects. In this respect, art materials become a tool in which intellectually understood concepts can be strengthened. That is, in order for a child to draw or paint his ideas, he has to rethink what he has just experienced. This causes him to re-focus his mental images on the ideas which have stimulated a particular mode of thought. Basically, *intellectual motivations emphasize the acquisition and development of factual knowledge* as it pertains to himself, to others, or to objects in question. Knowledge is not a by-product of art expression, but it is a necessary prerequisite. Unless a child learns specific facts concerning people, animals, birds, flowers, and so forth, he will not be able to say very much about them in his art. If for instance the teacher asks a child to draw a picture of a bird the child is unlikely to say very much about birds unless he has learned specific information concerning them. The teacher can be assured of a much richer concept in terms of pictures, if the child's thinking is directed to

Seeking interesting patterns, shapes, and textures helps in the development of design concepts.

factual information concerning birds. This could be accomplished by bringing a live bird to class, showing a good film, or taking a trip to the zoo. Here is a sample motivation using an intellectually oriented discussion:

Learning About Characteristics of Birds

Materials. Paints, brushes or crayons, paper 18″ x 24″.

Sample Intellectual Motivation. For our art learning time this morning, I am looking for someone who can tell the class what he knows about birds. There's a hand. Bobby knows something, Rosie knows . . . Good! Already, many of you know something about birds. Yes, they can fly. Yes, they have two legs, feathers, wings, a beak . . . (At this point, you could introduce some live birds, or a film, or many illustrative pictures, or provide a firsthand experience by going to a pet shop or zoo.) As the children observe and examine the birds, the questions could become *much more* specific and detailed, such as:

How do birds move their wings to fly?
What shape are the feathers?
Are they all the same size?
What are the legs like?
Are they jointed?
How does the bird hold himself on a twig?
Are all birds the same color?
How does a bird bend to eat a worm?
What is the bird's mouth like?
Can birds talk?
Would you like to be a bird?
How would you feel up high on a tree limb?
Did you ever touch a bird? Do they feel like a kitten?
Do birds have different types of beaks? Why?

These questions should not be asked in rapid-fire sequence but should be interspersed throughout the stimulation time. When the children have learned some facts concerning birds, it is then possible to provide them with an opportunity to draw or paint what they have learned.

Here are some additional topics for intellectual motivations:

Figure: Learning what eyes are like
How the mouth chews
What ears can do
Where the body bends
How we run
All about fingers

Insects: Grasshoppers (How do they hop?)
Ants (How many eyes? Do they chew?)
Crickets (How do they sing?)
Bees (How do they collect nector?)
Butterflies (Where do they come from?)

Animals: Cows (Udders, hoofs, horns, stomach)
Horses (Do they have teeth?)
Dogs (Is their fur soft?)
Cats (How do they arch their backs?)
Rats (Are they really sneaky?)
Bats (Do they have eyes?)

Plants: Learning about trees (leaves, bark, roots)
How flowers are different
How do grapes grow?
What makes corn-on-the-cob?
How do vegetables grow?

Any object can be suitable for an intellectual motivation. We want to teach children to perceive the details of these things. We also want them to relate themselves in some way to the items. Intellectual motivations serve two purposes: (1) They strengthen factual knowledge of things, and (2) they establish relationships between child and thing. For instance, learning details of what birds are like is factual. "Feeding the chickens," "Talking to the myna bird," or "Flying south" pertain to how the child establishes relationships with birds. Both types of experiences are necessary if a child is to express his ideas in an aesthetic manner. Art skill cannot develop if the child has never developed the necessary mental imagery.

Imaginative Motivations. Imaginative motivations are concerned with the development of a child's imagination, inventiveness, and originality. Within this motivational area, *creative thinking* has an opportunity to grow. In *imaginative motivations, the main emphasis is on developing uniqueness of idea*. These motivations should stress individual idea-skills and unusual solutions to problems.

What we should look for in this motivational category are ideas which are less conventional and less bound to routine thinking. In this respect, teachers and parents must learn to accept from children all ideas which may seem *odd-ball* or different from the standard. In fact, *odd-ball* is exactly the term we want to start using in this particular approach. That is, we are looking for motivations which in themselves will stimulate a variety of new possibilities for art problem solutions. The *odd-ball approach* can enable us to break through conventional patterns and rules and can thus encourage a uniquely new type of fundamental thinking. Ideas which might have seemed silly and ridiculous now have an opportunity to fit into motivations and experiences which employ *odd-ball* methods for stimulating creative thinking. *Odd-ball* motivations are not bound to the traditional methods of using art materials. In this respect, the individual is less defensive, and more apt to be flexible during the working process.

Here are some suggestions for stimulating thinking in an imaginative vein. Many of these ideas are strictly *odd-ball* in approach:

Inventing a nonsense machine
Walking around the other side of the moon
Turning into an insect
If you were the tallest person on earth
If you were invisible
Replacing your head with something else
Growing wings
Swallowing things whole
Turning into a monster
Shrinking to microscopic size
Becoming the last person on earth

We are concerned here with what happens to increase a person's inventiveness through exploring such unusual directions. Listed following is a sample problem relating to an *odd-ball* or nonsense machine:

Inventing a Nonsense Machine

Sample Imaginative Motivation. All of us have seen and know what regular machines can do. Some wrap packages, others shape rockets, auto parts, and silverware. Machines can do many, many things. I am thinking of some very special machines. These machines do nothing useful or practical. In fact, they are quite silly machines. I call one an automatic pea-picker. Another is a self-operating hair comber, and another is an automatic pickpocket. It is exciting to imagine ideas like this, and it helps us to think in less conventional ways. If you were going to construct a machine that did nothing useful, what would you think of? These questions will help to get you started on an idea:

Individuals should be stimulated by motivations of a less conventional nature in order to break down established barriers which previously stalled inventive thinking.

Can you wind it up?

Will there be a trigger release of some sort?

Will you operate it by hand?

Will there be a surprise element involved?

How will you make the wheels and pulleys turn?

Do you have to think of balance?

Will there be levers, gears, and pulleys?

Will all the wheels turn at the same time?

Can you crank it?

Perhaps we should collect a number of scrap items first and then develop our ideas from what we find. Here is a list of materials that might prove helpful to you. Add as many more as you can find:

String	Paper
Rubber bands	Beads
Toy wheels	Sticks
Gears	Spools
Old tinkertoy and erector set parts	Wire
	Nails
Thumbtacks	Nuts and bolts
Glass	Washers
Stones	and many more things that
Glue	you discover

References

Bannon, Laura, *Mind Your Child's Art,* New York: Pelligrini and Cudahy, 1952.

Carter, Bruce, "Artistic Development and Auditory Sensitivity: An Initial Study," *Research in Art Education,* Eastern Arts Association, Vol. 14, No. 5, May, 1957.

Cole, Natalie Robinson, *The Arts in the Classroom,* New York: The John Day Company, 1940.

D'Amico, Victor, and Frances Wilson, *Art for the Family,* New York: Museum of Modern Art, 1956.

Herberholz, Barbara, "Christmas Motivation," *School Arts,* November, 1959.

Herberholz, Donald, "An Experimental Study to Determine the Effect of Modeling on the Drawing of the Human Figure by Second Grade Children," *National Art Education Association Yearbook,* 1957.

Herberholz, Donald, "Imagination Makes the Difference," *School Arts,* February, 1962.

Herberholz, Donald, "Stimulation by Film," *School Arts,* Vol. 62, No. 4, pp. 25-26, December, 1962.

Keiler, Manfred, *Art in the Schoolroom,* Lincoln, Nebraska: University of Nebraska Press, 1955.

Keiler, Manfred, "Some Thoughts on Motivation," *Everyday Art,* Vol. 37, pp. 12-17, Fall Issue, 1958.

Keiler, Manfred, "Motivation versus Stimulation," *Art Education, Journal of the National Art Education Asociation,* Vol., 411, No. 9, December, 1959, pp. 6-74.

Linderman, Earl W., "Figure Drawing as a Personal Style," *School Arts,* October, 1962.

Linderman, Earl W., "Idea-Tracking in the Classroom Teacher," *Art Education, Journal of the National Art Education Association,* January, 1963, Vol. XVI.

McVitty, Lawrence, "An Experimental Study on Various Methods in Art Motivation at the Fifth Grade Level," *National Art Education Association Yearbook,* 1956.

Viola, Wilhelm, *Child Art and Franz Cizek,* New York: Reynal & Company, 1936.

When the artist is alive in any person, whatever his kind of work may be, he becomes an inventive, searching, daring, self-expressing creature. He becomes interesting to other people. He disturbs, upsets, enlightens, and he opens ways for a better understanding. Where those who are not artists are trying to close the book, he opens it, shows there are still more pages possible.

The world would stagnate without him, and the world would be beautiful with him; for he is interesting to himself and he is interesting to others. He does not have to be a painter or sculptor to be an artist. He can work in any medium. He simply has to find the gain in the work itself, not outside it.

Robert Henri
from *The Art Spirit*
Philadelphia: J. B. Lippincott Co., 1923, p. 5

Chapter 5

Tools, Materials and Things Needed to Start to Work in Art

The beginning of a work of art may come from one or many directions at once. These beginnings might include sensory perceptions, feelings, experiences, ideas, images in the mind, tools or materials. The initial phase might come from any combination of these or any one; or it might start with one and shift back and forth rather often. A tool and how to use it might start a train of thought that could be pursued for several weeks. The same might be true of an art material or any material in our environment that we find stimulating to our senses or feelings. Enumerating a list of tools that could be used to paint with often "opens up" many ideas for an art activity or art investigation. The following list of tools might be used to push or move paint around on a surface:

Tools With Which To Paint

The tool might be hard or soft, fat or thin, narrow or wide, round or flat, long or short, rough or smooth. All of these words could suggest many materials.

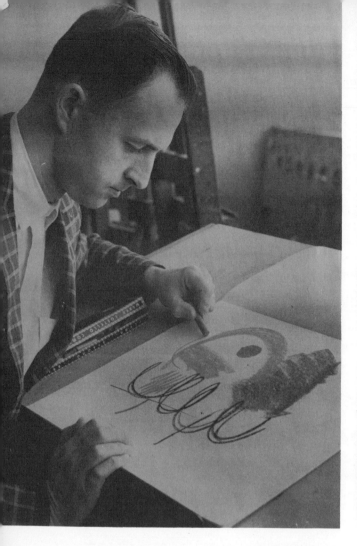

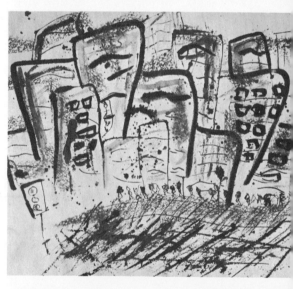

An essential aspect of art development is learning to use art materials in unique and unusual ways. Being open to the possibility of how tools can be used stimulates greater flexibility in their use.

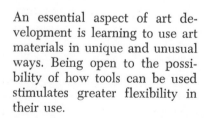

Have you ever tried to paint with:

fingers	rope
sticks	feathers
blocks of wood	rags
branches	rags tied to a stick
brushes:	sponges cut into many shapes
bottle brush	toothpicks
house brush	plastic dispenser bottles
paste brush	dish scrapers
solder brush	brayers
soft hairs	
hard bristle	
rubberized bristle	

An individual's perceptual openness may not allow him at first to think of these tools as "brushes." They are not brushes but they all serve the purpose of the idea of a brush—that is they allow the person to put the paint on the painting surface and allow the paint to be moved around, to be spread thick or thin, to be textured, to be blended, or to be put into shapes and lines. The use of such tools as these in painting will do much to develop awareness as to what can be done with paint as well as to an investigation of the tools. Combining different tools offers an almost endless number of experiments and experiences for the beginner and the mature artist.

We might also think of these tools in relation to a definite idea or expression of an experience. You might ask yourself what tool could be used to paint a picture that would create a feeling of lightness and airiness, or softness and delicateness, or freshness and crispness, or make a sparkling surface like wet grass. What tool would give the softness of fur, which one the roughness of rocks, which one would give powerful lines, angular shapes, and which one would give the splash of sloppy

tracks on the paper? These are all things tools can do. There are many ways to use tools which we discover as we work with them. We should always try to have many experiences with each in order to develop not only a fluency and flexibility but also a *depth* of experience in a few of them. Which one will we discover to be our special tool?

When painting a tree, we might ask ourselves what tool could best be used to paint the roots that go deep into the earth? What tool could be used to paint the stretching up of the branches? What tool could best suggest the smooth or rough bark of the trunk? What tool could suggest the delicate bud or fragile blossom? What tool could be used to suggest the moving leaves in the wind of early summer? What tool could be used to indicate the snow heavy on the branches, or the strong contrast of light or dark on the branches after a rain, or sharp pine needles, or soft blossoms of the poplar in the spring? These are some suggested ways to think of trees in relation to tools. The selection of the proper tool or tools can lead to a more successful expression of an idea, perception, or feeling.

Tools With Which To Draw

Drawing tools might be thought of as instruments to inscribe or mark on surfaces.

Have you ever tried to draw with:

crayons	felt tip pens	twigs
pencils	toothpicks	soap
fingers	bamboo	soldering wire
chalk	bones	nails
charcoal	straws	sticks
ink pens	feathers	

Depending on our background we may not be able to think of a thing to draw on with a bone, let alone what kind of a

Each art material used has a quality unique in itself. Through search and experimentation, the individual learns to release such qualities within his art expression.

mark a bone would make or what could be done with solder in relation to drawing. A great number of these materials may seem "odd" at first and we may not be able to think of them as drawing instruments. It has been found that when a person has not experienced the tool previously that he is likely to approach it with more openness and therefore be more creative and inventive in its use.

Most people would have difficulty in trying to think of a new way to use a pencil in drawing. It is generally used to make lines and shading. It has also been used by the average person to write with for a number of years, and as a result he is so familiar with it that he is "blinded" by past experiences in relation to its other possible uses. He tends to miss the silver-gray lines as well as the black ones. In contrast, the average person would be more alert to the possibilities of drawing with a tool to which he has not become "dulled." For instance, how would we draw with a toothpick, a twig, a feather, a pipe cleaner, or a nail? One might have to go through a line of thinking such as the following to discover the uses of these tools. Will I have to sharpen it, burn it, wet it, tie it together, hit it with another tool or break it before I can mark with it? Will I have to use a liquid with it? What kind of consistency should the liquid have? What kinds of surfaces will the tool mark on? Will specific materials or surfaces be more suitable for certain tools than others? This line of questioning about odd or unusual tools develops more possibilities for awareness. Conventional tools such as pencils, pens, and brushes will be more difficult to use with flexibility, fluency, or inventiveness.

Surfaces on Which To Draw or Paint

The surface might be absorbent or nonabsorbent, shiny or dull, smooth or rough, hard or soft, wet or dry, flexible or nonflexible, thick or thin. These are some of the things to consider when selecting a material or surface on which to paint or draw.

Have you ever tried to paint or draw on:

paper	cardboard
newsprint	corrugated
paper plates	pressed
paper bags	cloth
tissue paper	saran wrap
crepe paper	acetate
paper towels	aluminum foil
cellophane	masonite
carbon	sidewalks or driveways
butcher	back yard fences
waxed paper	chalkboards
wood	hard soil
stones	sand
glass	

One can experiment with any combination of painting tools, drawing tools, and surfaces on which they might be used. To experiment means to find out about how surfaces and tools interact with each other. It is assumed that through experimentation many new facts, ideas, and feelings about the tools and surfaces will be realized. The experiment should lead to a tentative conclusion and then another experiment and not be just a meaningless manipulation of materials. Through experimentation one should have a greater identity with the surfaces and tools and as a result be better able to predict their behavior.

Experience with tools and surfaces is very important to consider when thinking about an art activity. Children need not only stimulating ideas to work with but also stimulating tools and surfaces. They require materials and tools that permit exploration, arouse investigation, stimulate thinking, and are suitable for their stage of development. In fact a child may need several lessons concerning the use of a tool or surface before he is ready to express ideas. Poor expression often is due to lack of identification with the behavior of the tool or surface. The older child will require more detailed instruction in the procedures of painting and drawing.

Suggestions for Using Unusual Tools To Draw and Paint With on Unusual Surfaces

What ideas could you paint using a manila rope the size of your thumb and aluminum foil or corrugated cardboard as a painting surface?

Have you ever tried painting on soft sugar pine with water colors?

Have you ever tried drawing with crayons on a weathered board from an old building or an old fence?

What tools could be used to draw or paint with on tissue paper?

Would you use a pencil, crayon, finger, stick, straw, feather, toothpick, bamboo, bone, or nail to draw in the hard earth with? What could you use to color it with?

What tools could you use to make marks on glass? What liquids would adhere to glass? Could you mark through these liquids after they are dry?

When you think of branches as a painting tool do you think of one or many? Is it possible to make a tool of several smaller branches so that many marks could be made with one stroke?

What kind of marks could you make with a bar of soap? On what kind of surfaces would you be able to make these marks?

Could you draw a line with the tip of a feather?

Liquids With Which To Draw or Paint

Liquids used in drawing or painting might be thought of as those that remain basically on the surface or those that stain or penetrate the surface to which they are applied. The liquids might be thought of as opaque or transparent.

Have you ever tried to paint with:

water colors	food dyes	bleach
poster paints	liquid shoe polish	liquid wax
muddy water	melted crayons	glue
corn syrup	rubber cement	condensed milk
india ink	egg tempera	buttermilk
tea	rubber base enamels	
coffee	berry juices	

Exploring the combinations of painting and drawing tools, surfaces, and liquids will give one an almost endless list of possible experiments. These explorations and experiments should not only lead one to an enriched understanding of unusual or *odd-ball* materials but should reopen the senses to conventional art materials.

Surprise Procedures With Materials

These are methods that can be used that withhold the final product or those where accidents occur in the process.

Print making is the leader in this area of art work. Waiting to see what the final result will be is a real thrill that shouldn't be missed. After a person has finished cutting the block he doesn't know what it will look like until it is printed. The same is true of a monoprint, glue print, soap, or plasticene print. In the monoprint the drawing is made first on the plate or the back of the paper that has been placed on the inked plate but it is not until the paper is removed that one can see what has been accomplished.

Sand casting is another "surprise" procedure. It might be called three-dimensional print making. The process of cutting or imprinting into the sand makes it very similar to a linoleum block cut. In fact one can make a cast of a linoleum block cut.

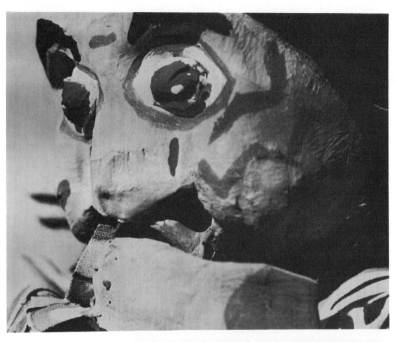

Concepts may evolve from many different materials. It is more t h e i n d i v i d u a l' s a w a r e n e s s of the uniqueness of the material that enables him to discover its potential.

Photo, Courtesy: "Everyday Art" Magazine, The American Crayon Company.

When the individual identifies completely with the material, the art product is produced. The process is then repeated again and again, and the individual matures aesthetically.

Blottos and rubber cement on paper are two more procedures of this type that always provide one with a successful experience.

All of the surprise procedures or those that contain a surprise element are usually successful with the child or adult whether he be a beginner or an advanced student. The products produced in these procedures are usually asethetically pleasing to the one who produces them.

How many more "surprise" techniques can we think of?

Some Approaches to Discovering Color and Textures

In combining tools and materials the teacher or child should have some experiences with color and textures. Most people are responsive to *color* and it is a good element to start with.

To discover color one might try:

dropping colors onto a wet surface and allowing them to run together;

dripping melted crayons;

looking through a prism;

making a crayon etching;

looking at a color against a white background and removing it to see the afterimage;

using poster paint on black construction paper;

using sponge and overlay poster paint colors;

putting colors on a folded piece of paper and pressing it so the colors run;

dropping different colors of ink or food coloring into a glass of water;

placing tissues or cellophane over each other to mix colors.

These are all ways that give quick results, are exciting to view, and can be accomplished by any age group.

To discover textures one might make crayon or brayer prints of different surfaces around the house and then use the textured paper for cutting and pasting a picture. Various textures can be combined in a collage (how many soft textures can we collect; how many smooth, shiny, rough, fuzzy?) Gadget prints and blottos help one discover the texture qualities of paint. Rubbing the side of the crayon on paper will bring out the texture of the paper. Print making brings out the textures one can make with a tool on linoleum or wood. The textures made with our fingers or a tool in clay can better be realized after the impression has been cast in plaster. Look through a reading glass or magnifying glass at textures. See how many different textures can be collected from a magazine. See how many similar textures can be found in real objects. All of these will be ways to enrich our knowledge about the two and three dimensional textures of things that surround us every day.

Many different ways have been suggested to help one get started in an art activity and here are a few more to consider. The following are types of things that might help a person become involved in a creative art activity. They tell how to follow a procedure or how to look for the details of things in our environment. They can stimulate imagination through words, pictures, and sounds.

Here is a list of games, self-starting art activities, books, records, films, and things that teachers should find stimulating enough to guide them to more creative ways of thinking. Through looking, listening, thinking, and doing, we can increase our knowledge about art.

Books

Betts, Victoria B., *Exploring Papier Mâché*, Worcester, Mass.: The Davis Press, 1955.

Bland, Jane Cooper, *Art for the Family*, New York: The Museum of Modern Art, 1957.

Borten Helen, *A Picture Has a Special Look,* New York: Abelard-Schuman, 1961.

Brooks, Leonard, *Water Color, a Challenge,* New York: Reinhold Publishing Co., 1957.

Budney, Blosom, *A Kiss Is Round,* New York: Lothrop, Lee and Shepard Co., 1954.

Emberley, Ed, *The Wing of a Flea,* Boston: Little, Brown, and Co., 1961.

Fearing, Kelley, and others, *Our Expanding Vision,* Books One to Eight, Austin, Texas: W. S. Benson and Co., 1960.

Field Enterprises, Inc., *Art for Children,* Childcraft Vol. 10, Chicago, 1954.

Garbaty, Norman, *Print Making with a Spoon,* New York: Reinhold Publishing Co., 1960.

Highland, Harold, *The How and Why Wonder Book of Light and Color,* New York: Wonder Books, 1963.

Keen, Martin, *The How and Why Wonder Book of the Microscope and What You See,* New York: Wonder Books, 1961.

Keiler, Manfred, *The Art in Teaching Art,* Lincoln, Nebraska: University of Nebraska Press, 1961.

Lionni, Leo, *Inch by Inch,* New York: Ivan Oblensky, Inc., 1960.

Lord, Lois, *Collage and Construction,* Worchester, Mass.: Davis Publications, Inc., 1958.

Loughran, Bernice B., *Art Experiences, An Experimental Approach,* New York: Harcourt, Brace and World, 1963.

MacAgy, Douglas and Elizabeth, *Going for a Walk with a Line,* Garden City, New York: Doubleday & Co., 1959.

Marks, Mickey Klar, *Sand Sculpturing,* New York: The Dial Press, 1962.

Mattil, Edward L., *Meaning in Crafts,* Englewood Cliffs, N.J.: Prentice-Hall, Inc., 1962.

O'Neill, Mary, *Hailstones and Halibut Bones, Adventures in Color,* Garden City, New York: Doubleday and Co., Inc., 1961.

Ota, Koshi, *Printing for Fun,* New York: McDowell, Obolensky, Inc., 1959.

Reed, Carl, and Joseph Orze, *Art from Scrap,* Worchester, Mass.: Davis Publications, Inc., 1960.

Reid, Alastair, *Ounce, Dice, Trice,* Boston: Little, Brown and Co., 1958.

Wankelman, Willard and others, *Arts and Crafts for Elementary Teachers,* Dubuque, Iowa: Wm. C. Brown Co., 1954.

Wankelman, Willard and others, *A Handbook of Arts and Crafts,* Dubuque, Iowa: Wm. C. Brown Co., 1961.

Weiss, Harvey, *Paper, Ink and Roller,* New York: Young Scott Books, 1958.

Weiss, Harvey, *Clay, Wood and Wire,* New York: William R. Scott, Inc., 1956.

Records

A Child's Introduction to Patriotism, The Collegiate Chorale, Wonderland Records.

Glazer, Tom, and Paul Tripp, *Why, Mommy?,* Harmony LP Columbia Records.

Hample, Stoo, *The Silly Record,* Columbia Records.

Hunter, Kim, and others, *From Morning 'Til Night and a Bag Full of Poems,* RCA Victor.

Ives, Burl, *Little White Duck and Other Children's Favorites,* Columbia Harmony Records.

McCurdy, Ed, and others, *Folk Songs from the Children's Zoo,* Riverside Wonderland Records.

Saint-Saens, Camille, *Carnival of the Animals,* Wonderland Records.

Singing Science Records, Science Materials Center, Inc., 220 23rd St., New York 10, N.Y. (series of 6).

Things

Early Childhood Discovery, catalog, Creative Playthings Inc., Princeton, N.J.

Picture Printer, designed by Arnold Arnold, Salem, Mass.: Pastime Products, a division of Parker Brothers, Inc.

Science Materials Center, Inc., catalog, 220 East 23rd Street, New York 10, N.Y.

Story Drawing Set, a Self-starting Art Activity, designed by Arnold Arnold, Salem Mass.: Pastime Products, a division of Parker Brothers, Inc.

Table Top Workshop, designed by Arnold Arnold, Salem, Mass.: Pastime Products, a division of Parker Brothers, Inc.

The Poetry-Drawing Book, edited by William Cole and Julia Colmore, New York: Simon and Schuster, 1962.

The Second Poetry-Drawing Book, edited by William Cole and Julia Colmore, New York: Simon and Schuster, 1962.

Art is an intellectual and an emotional recording of an attitude or an experience presented in a personal manner. The visual arts—painting, sculpture, architecture, and other related arts—are concerned with the creative handling of lines, textures, shapes, colors and space in materials such as paint, stone, and wood. "Creative" implies bringing into existence new constructions through a personal arrangement of existing or new elements.

James A. Schinneller
from *Art: Search and Self-Discovery,*
Scranton: International Textbook Co.,
1961, page 2

Chapter 6

Starting a Beginning Art Program

Planning Art Lessons

For the person who has seldom taught art or who needs a stronger foundation in teaching art to children, here are several suggestions to consider in starting a regular classroom art program:

1. Plan at least one period each week in which to present art motivations to the class. Plan each art lesson carefully and know what the objectives will be.

2. Plan at least one period every two weeks for discussing fine, original works of art. This could include paintings, sculpture, print making, ceramics, jewelry, weaving, and many other art media. Encourage the children to discuss *what* and *how* they feel about the art works.

3. Develop an art-beauty corner where children can be encouraged to bring in beautiful objects and pictures they discover at home. Provide some time for the children to discuss their discoveries which might range from snow-white daisies to a collection of patterned stones.

Artists use various materials to express ideas. They try to select materials which will best correspond to their mental images.

4. Provide an exhibit space where original art works can be attractively displayed. Very often local art collectors will be happy to loan interesting art objects. Other sources include art galleries, high school and college art departments, and private collections of art teachers.

5. Bring guest artists to the classroom for discussion and demonstration of how they develop their art works.

6. Encourage the children to start a file collection of beautiful and interesting pictures. Classifications might range from "artists we learned about" to "exciting ideas we discovered through pictures."

7. Plan several trips a year for taking the children to an art gallery. Make them planned experiences in which the children look for specific objectives rather than wander aimlessly from room to room.[1]

8. Another positive approach to art experiences is to have each child make an "art learning" notebook. Information and knowledge of what they learn about art can be added to the notebook. The notebook could be divided into several parts such as (1) art terms, (2) artists we learned about, (3) art materials we have explored and know, (4) ideas we have learned through art, and (5) what we have learned about design.

Outline for Developing a Beginning Art Program

A very important first step in organizing a beginning art program is to plan a tentative outline which can be used as a working guide. It need be only as elaborate as one has resources to make it. Here is a suggested outline.

---

[1]Linderman, Earl W., "Child Art and the Teacher," *Grade Teacher*, April, 1962.

I. *Components of a basic art program*

1. Art as developing readiness for awareness is basic to the development of any creative expression by the child. (These components are discussed in Chapter 2).

2. Art as *creative experience* should be recognized as a means of developing the child's *artistic, intellectual,* and *imaginative* faculties through definite art motivations. (These components are discussed in Chapter 4).

3. Art as *skill development* is an important part of the child's art growth. While most children will not become artists, all children should begin to learn the values of working as skillfully and carefully as possible. Skills in art processes consist of learning to use and care for appropriate art materials and discovering the potentiality of art media through exploration and experimentation (These components are discussed in Chapter 5).

4. Art as *study and appreciation* should emphasize the value of learning about art in terms of specific subject matter. With these objectives stated, it is now possible to amplify our fourth component.

Art As Study and Appreciation

Classroom teachers may feel somewhat reluctant to teach the subject of art because of their own lack of familiarity with the field. It should be remembered however that any unit of learning may seem strange at first. Having the courage to take the initial plunge will soon prove to be as exciting for teachers as students—and both can learn together. Here's how to begin:

The first step is to organize a plan by which the vast subject of art can be reduced into smaller, workable categories. Most libraries contain a fine selection of art books which offer a variety of information. Jot down on a paper the various subject areas of art that come to mind. It doesn't matter where one begins since the launching of the program is the vital step. The

Where can we find art sources in our community? Some sources include public galleries, private galleries, college art departments, and artist studios. Some galleries provide a rental service in which individuals can select fine, original art works for display in the home.

Barrios Gallery, Sacramento, California.

Crocker Art Gallery, Sacramento, California.

Courtesy: Crocker Art Gallery, Sacramento, California.

Rental day at the Crocker Art Gallery, Sacramento, California.

Art gallery directors and teachers can help us increase our understanding and appreciation of art. They do this by planned discussions and tours for groups as well as individual criticism of paintings.

"City of Hope," water color,
William Kasza.

Sculpture in wood,
Harlan Hoffa.

"Tower Bridge," water color, Setsuo Kirinoe.

"River Scene," chalk drawing, Robert Else.

"Fighting Bird," water color, wax and
ink, Marlene Linderman.

Artists work in various styles.
When the ideas of artist and
viewer coincide, aesthetic understanding takes place.

Oil by Frank Borge.

information obtained can be adapted to a specific grade level. For example, here is a beginning plan for developing an initial art program:

Step One, following, consists of selecting and listing the over-all general units intended for art study.

STEP ONE (GENERAL CLASSIFICATIONS OF ART UNITS):

Classification A: FINE ARTS
Unit   I—Painting
       II—Sculpture
       III—Drawing
       IV—Print making

Classification B: CRAFTS
Unit   I—Weaving
       II—Ceramics
       III—Jewelry

Classification C: DESIGN
Unit   I—Elements of Design
       II—Fashion Design
       III—Advertising Design
       IV—Industrial Design

Classificiation D: ARCHITECTURE
Unit   I—Homes
       II—Commercial Structures
       III—Landscapes and Parks

From a general over-all subject plan such as this, it is possible to elaborate more fully. For instance, Step Two consists of selecting each of the foregoing units and then deciding which type of information and approach would best suit the needs of a particular class. Once the material has been organized for each specific subject unit, the next procedure would be to outline the material for future class presentation. From the general classifications and units presented in Step One, a more detailed approach might be planned something like Step Two.

STEP TWO (UNIT CLARIFICATION)

Unit   I—Painting
    1. *Different types of artists*
      a. Realistic artists—tell us stories of everyday experiences.
      b. Landscape artists—paint pictures of scenery.
      c. Abstract artists—paint things in new ways.
      d. Portrait artists—paint pictures of people.
      e. Imaginative artists—tell us of make-believe events.

    2. *Materials of the artists*
      a. Water color paint
      b. Oil paint
      c. Brushes
      d. Varnish
      e. Casein
      f. Papers
      g. Turpentine
      h. Canvas

Each unit of the art program could be planned in a manner similar to the foregoing. In this way, vast amounts of information will not become unwieldy. Step Three consists of further clarification in terms of the subject unit.

STEP THREE (DETAILED ANALYSIS)

Unit   I—Painting (Further breakdown on artists)
    Realistic Artists
    1. Definition of realistic artists—There are artists who like to tell us ideas of everyday life. Realistic artists paint pictures which tell us stories

of people, animals, flowers, trees, trucks, trains, airplanes, and many other everyday things.

2. *American artists who have painted stories of everyday life:*

Edward Hopper	Andrew Wyeth
John Sloan	Thomas Benton
Albert Ryder	Grant Wood
Charles Burchfield	Phillip Evergood
Dong Kingman	Ben Shahn
George Bellows	Maurice Prendergast

3. *Artists from other countries who have painted stories of everyday life:*

Auguste Renoir	Georges Seurat
Claude Monet	Paul Cézanne
Francisco Goya	Honoré Daumier
Maurice Utrillo	Camille Pissaro
Edgar Degas	

As the outline proceeds, each step along the way should become consistently more detailed in terms of the study unit. Each step should also be expanded in terms of what preceded it in the previous successive steps. The outline here is by no means complete or otherwise extensive, but it is presented to provide a beginning plan from which the teacher can begin to develop her own art program.

Art Terms We Learn About

In any art program there are many terms which must be defined in order to develop a language of art. Once this language has been learned, communication between individuals is enriched. Listed are some typical art terms which teachers and children can learn. When the children have become familiar with these terms, many more can be added to the list. These can be readily included in the children's art notebooks.

Art Terms

ABSTRACT: Simplified version, usually not representational.

ACCENT: Specific areas within a composition which are given greater emphasis by the use of more intense tone, size change, or other means which exaggerate these specific parts.

AESTHETIC: A term referring to the fine arts or to art forms in which the "beautiful" or artistic qualities of forms are given consideration.

ANALAGOUS COLORS: Colors which are closely related to each other, and in which a common hue can be found e.g., blue, blue-violet, violet.

ARMATURE: Framework made of wire or wood and used to support the structure of a form in claywork, papier-mâché, or other modeling techniques.

ASYMMETRICAL BALANCE: (Informal balance) Unequal distribution of art elements resulting in a visually pleasing balance.

BALANCE:A visual impression of equilibrium between all interactive parts in any art work.

BRAYER: Rubber or gelatin roller used in printing to spread ink evenly over a surface.

BUTCHER PAPER: Glossy paper which usually comes in large rolls suitable for mural work.

CANVAS: A coarse, heavy cloth of hemp, linen or cotton used as a surface for oil painting.

CALLIGRAPHY: Refers to the use of line in varying widths and rhythms as commonly used in brush lettering.

CARTOON: A preliminary drawing for a painting or mural.

"General Lilliput Tip-toeing through the Tulips," pastel and ink, Earl Linderman.

"Medusa," stitchery, Jean Ray Laury.

"Auburn Diggings," oil, David Dangelo.

"Woman," sculpture, Georgiane Else.

"Waiting the Day," linoleum print, Don Uhlin.

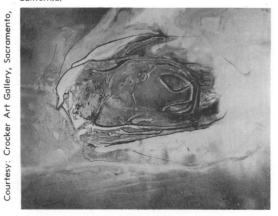

"Submerged Bird," oil, Don Reich.

Artists living today produce many styles which are personal to them. Artists throughout history have produced art in various styles.

"Christ Healing the Blind," School of Van Dyck.

"Suits of Japanese Armor."

"Young Mason Eating Dinner," Bernhard Reinhold.

The artist is a spokesman in society. His reasons for painting specific ideas are closely related to his experiences and thinking.

CARVING: The act of designing by cutting away parts of a surface, such as stone or wood.

CERAMICS: A term standing for objects made from clay and then fired.

COLLAGE: An arrangement of various materials such as cloth, wood, paper, and various scraps, into a visually pleasing art form. The method used is pasting.

COLOR: Usually thought of as the hues found in a spectrum in which wave lengths of light are diffused into the various colors by their reflection against surfaces.

COMPLEMENTARY COLORS: Refers to colors which are opposite each other on a standard color wheel, i.e., red and green, orange and blue.

COMPOSITION: The arrangement and organization of parts into a unified whole in which all parts unite to form a new total relationship.

CONTOUR: The outer surface of an object or figure, usually bounded by a line, change of color, or change of texture.

DESIGN: The skillful ordering and building of artistic thoughts into visual expressions with art media.

ETCHING: A method of engraving a design on a copper or zinc plate by means of acid. From this plate a "print" is made.

FORM: The finished product as it appears after the art elements have been arranged and completed.

FREE-FORM: A shape which has no fixed or rigid boundaries.

FRESCO: Painting done on moist plaster in which the pigments become incorporated with the plaster.

GOUACHE: Refers to opaque water colors.

HARMONY: Occurs when all of the art elements have been organized into a visually pleasing relationship.

ILLUSTRATION: Refers to an art product in which the story content is clearly evident.

INTENSITY: Refers to the amount of pigment in a color. Bright colors contain considerable amounts of pigment.

LINE: The path made by a moving point. It can vary in width, direction, and length.

LITHOGRAPHY: Refers to the printing of an image on a surface material using a stone plate and a grease pencil.

LOST WAX PROCESS: Method of casting objects in metal which have been made from clay or other plastic materials.

MASS: The combination of several forms within an art work to form a larger body.

MEDIA: The art materials to be used.

MOBILE: A hanging, three-dimensional design which has moving parts.

MAT: A heavy border of paper or cardboard used to frame a drawing or painting.

MOUNT: To place, paste, or attach on a suitable support or backing. It enriches the visual appearance of an art work.

OIL PAINT: Pigment in linseed, poppy or nut oil.

PASTEL: Ground pigment that is combined with gum arabic and used in solid form. Colors are often tinted in appearance.

PERSPECTIVE: The art of creating an illusion of depth on a two dimensional surface. A visual method of drawing objects as they appear to our eye.

PICTURE PLANE: Refers to the surface on which the artist makes his drawing, painting, or design.

PRIMARY COLORS: These are thought of as the basic colors. They are red, yellow, and blue.

POSTER PAINT: Opaque paint, in dry or liquid form, suitable for classroom use.

PROPORTION: May refer to size relationships within an art work, or may refer to quantities of tone or color.

RELIEF: In sculpture, the exposure of certain parts away from a base or foundation.

RHYTHM: A regulated flow of colors, lines, textures, or other art elements to achieve a pleasing effect.

SHAPE: Can be geometric or free-form in dimension and is defined by a line or color area.

SPECTRUM: A band of colors deprived from wave lengths of light when seen through a prism or other reflective material.

STILL LIFE: Any combination of objects, such as fruits, books, vases, that the artist arranges for use as subject matter.

STYLE: The manner in which an individual artist approaches his work; his particular method of working, applying pigment to a surface, carving, modeling, etc.

SYMBOL: Something which stands for or represents the actual image or idea.

TACTILE: Refers to the sense of touch.

TEXTURE: The visual or surface feel of an object to our touch or vision.

TEMPERA: See Poster Paint.

VALUE: Refers to the lightness or darkness of a color.

VITREOUS: Refers to high fire ceramic ware such as porcelain. This material is glassy and nonporous.

WASH: A watered down pigment which causes a transparent effect when used over other lines or colors.

WEFT (WOOF): The thread used in weaving.

WARP: The threads from which a loom is strung. These threads run lengthwise.

WEDGE: To cut and pound clay in order to prepare it for work in ceramics. This removes the air bubbles.
Have the children add more terms to this list.

Historical Summary of Art Development

The next section of the *art study and appreciation* program could include an historical overview of art. The subject is so expansive that each teacher must decide what information is pertinent to her specific class. As the children gain more fluency in their "art language," the teacher will be able to approach art units of study in greater detail. In the beginning it might be wise to begin the history of art in simple but concise terms. Here are the major highlights of art as it has grown and influenced western art since the dawn of history. An approach such as this will provide a reference point and procedural plan:

Prehistoric Art
(40,000-5000 B.C.)

Man's earliest attempts to represent his ideas and feelings in visual form have their origin in the pre-dawn of history. The first evidence of prehistoric artistic endeavor was discovered on the roof of Altimira cave located near Santander on the northern coast of Spain. The cave of Altimira and many sister caves in both Spain and France yielded great discoveries of beautifully painted animals. There were deer, boar, bisons, elephants, and many symbolic figures of man engaged in the hunt for survival—all painted by skilled artists who lived thousands of years ago. The artistry of these early people is evident not only in the cave paintings but in the simple stone and bone tools which they fashioned for utilitarian purposes. As seen from these earliest beginnings, man has indicated a special need to embellish his implements in order to create objects which contained elements of visual beauty as well as practicality.

"Head of Bearded Man," drawing, Peter Paul Rubens.

"Madonna and Child," polychromed wood, French, fourteenth century.

Some artists may paint religious themes while other artists may be concerned with anatomical figures. Still others paint landscapes.

"Three Trees," etching, Rembrandt.

"Landscape Near Rome," oil, Gaspard Dughet.

"San Marco Piazza, Venice," oil Antonio Canaletto.

"Gobelin's Tapestry," French, fifteenth century.

Some paintings are flat and decorative. Some are symbolic. Some are highly realistic, emphasizing perspective and chiaroscuro to create atmospheric effects.

Ancient Art
(4500-30 B.C.)

Ancient art extended through several cultures, some contemporary to each other in time. Many of these ancient civilizations occupied the area of the Mediterranean Sea, Middle East Asia, and extended as far as China and Japan. All told several of these societies left their mark on history, both in terms of recorded evidence of a people and as artistic achievement of an extremely magnificent stature. While it is almost impossible to pinpoint the entire picture of art at this time or to know precise dates, enough data has been and continues to be discovered to provide considerable insight into the artistic expression of these ancient peoples. The art forms of these ancient empires can be roughly chronicled in the following manner:

a. *Egyptian Art*—Egyptian art encompassed three major kingdoms.

They included the Old Kingdom, the Middle Kingdom, and the Empire. The artistry of the Old Kingdom was created in direct relation to the philosophy which Egyptians of nobility held toward life. Basically they believed that existence on Earth was preparatory to life hereafter. As a result the all-powerful pharoahs, who represented diety figures on Earth, had tombs erected to glorify and protect their Earth bodies during the time when they would begin their heavenly journeys. These tombs contained the essence of Egyptian man's artistic achievements. The pyramids of Giza are the most dramatic architectural feats of this period. These magnificent tombs contained stone sculptures, elaborately painted wall reliefs which depicted everyday life, pottery, jewelry, and many utilitarian remains contemporary to the time. The art of the Middle Kingdom and the Empire was characterized predominantly by elaborate temples erected in honor of the ruling emperors. The artistry of this age was present in these temples, in both architectural design and interior decoration. The artist was often directly involved with the architect and builders in the construction of such temples. The joint efforts of artist and architect are evident in the decorative colonnades and walled surfaces of the temples as well as the furniture and implements used in the interior of the structures. Sculptural forms were often united with structural support. The most famous of these temples were uncovered at Luxor and Karnak. During this period the Egyptians developed painting techniques to a highly proficient degree. Many of the other arts enjoyed great popularity during this period. Some of the most magnificent examples of metalwork, furniture design, pottery, and glassware have been attributed to this splendid age.

b. *Sumerian Art*—Sumerian art existed as a cultural expression in an historical time that roughly parallels Egyptian achievements. This Middle East nation lacked stone or wood in any quantity, thus the chief building material consisted of sundried brick from clay. The Sumerians built temples and palaces also, although they did not seem to be as preoccupied with life in the next world as they were with the here-and-now. Their most notable achievement in the construction of their palaces was a colorful tower known as a *ziggurat*. For the most part, Sumerian art reflects a society filled with vigor and artistic power. Their artistic achievements are notably evident in the temple relief sculpture, metalwork, and frescoed murals adorning the palace walls. The Sumerians developed a cuneiform system of writing, were accomplished builders (having explored the possibilities of the archway in architectural construction), and expanded their knowledge of glazed tiles for wall decoration.

c. *Assyrian Art*—The main flow of Assyrian art was accomplished from 1000 to 600 B.C. The Assyrian state was located at the northern end of the Tigris-Euphrates Valley in Middle East Asia. Their art was of a dynamic sort and depicted the militant and warlike nature of its people. Battle scenes, wounded animals, and monster figures are characteristic images found in their sculptural pieces and wall paintings. Many of the Assyrian art forms suggest traces of Sumerian art but on a much grander scale. Unlike the more traditional Egyptians with their highly stylized approach to art and life, the Assyrians expressed life with brusqueness and vigor. The most significant of their art treasures is to be found in their architecturally magnificent palaces which housed many fine sculptures and wall paintings.

d. *Persian Art*—Another ancient civilization which strongly influenced societies of this age was Persia. Some of the most exciting examples of woven and ceramic ware can be traced as far back as 5000 B.C. Persian rugs today reflect a style that continues to delight individuals around the world. Many of the art

"Italian Park," wash, Jean Honore Fragonard.

"Meeting on the Bridge," wood block print, Utagawa Hiroshige.

"St. Peter Liberated by the Angel," ink drawing, Rembrandt.

Paintings help to provide insight into our own experiences and the experiences of others.

works of these earlier civilizations have been lost to us forever, and rarer still are the names of the artists from these forgotten times.

e. *Greek Art*—The art of Greece began to flower around 600 B.C. The only remaining traces of their art in any quantity can be observed in their architectural and sculptural remains. Painting, although supposedly one of the their most vital arts, has been all but lost to us. Their ceramic wares indicate that painting was commonly employed as part of their artistic expression. Greek art, as a style, influenced the entire world at one time or another. The Romans borrowed it almost entirely. During the Middle Ages both the Romanesque and Gothic cathedrals drew upon the Greek influence.[2] Our cities today clearly depict several architectural landmarks from this ancient civilization. Some of the Greek sculptors are known to us. The most influential included Phidias, Myron, Praxiteles, Polyclitus, and Lysippus.

Art of the Middle Ages
(300 A.D. to 1300 A.D.)

This period of civilization is often referred to as the Dark Ages. Economic and social conditions were such that man had to devote the full measure of his time to the fight for survival. The church became the most important source of artistic achievement during this period. The monks in the various monasteries kept the glow of culture alive through their illuminated manuscripts which were finely decorated and painted. The *Book of Kells* from the eighth century monastery of the same name contains excellent examples of the art work unique to this period. Most of the art of this time was painted flatly in a decorative style. Figures were represented in a symbolic manner to suggest divine images. Understandably the art of this time was closely akin to the religious beliefs which prevailed. Christianity and art grew hand in hand during this age with the art forms reflecting the growing strength of the church. The flat handling of paint and the decorative style may have been influenced in part by a

---

[2]Sewall, John Ives., *A History of Western Art*, New York: Holt, Rinehart and Winston, 1961.

desire to discard the paganistic influences of Greece and Rome where realism and man were considered most vital.

Toward the end of the Middle Ages, particularly in the twelfth century, economic conditions improved to the point where old feudal systems began to deteriorate, thus paving the way for the growth of towns. Eventually, these towns became centers of learning with the church providing a strong influential leadership. A style of art known as *Gothic* developed, particularly in France and Germany, and is most evident today in the splendid cathedrals built to fit the needs of a deeply religious society. Unique innovations in architectural construction such as the "flying buttress" permitted the artist to employ vast amounts of stained glass for the wall surfaces. Consequently the artist developed his artistic expression through the use of stained glass which was ultimately wedded to the cathedral structure in a functional bond.

The Renaissance in Italy
(1300 A.D. to 1600 A.D.)

The Renaissance, which means a new birth, was the result of a rediscovery of the classical art and ideas of Greece coupled with a revolt from the flat, decorative symbolic style of art prevalent during the Gothic period. It is perhaps one of the greatest periods in the world history of art development. Many of our present day influences concerning art have their beginnings in the style of art that was developed during this time. Two of the most notable achievements in art which date from this period include the discovery of *perspective* (the illusion of depth on a two-dimensional surface), and *chiaroscuro* (the development of form through the use of light and dark). Both of these discoveries are key factors in the growth of a realistic style of art. Renaissance art is dotted with several great figures in painting and sculpture. The earliest to note was Giotto, who is said to have paved the pathway for those who came later. Giotto is respected as highly today as he probably was during his lifetime. The most noted artists of the Early Renaissance included such artists as Donatello (a sculptor), Masaccio, Fra Angelico, Botticelli, Fra Filippo Lippi, and Pollaiuolo. The High Renaissance gave birth to such masters as Leonardo DaVinci, Michelangelo, Raphael, Tinteretto, Giorgione, and Titian. Florence and Venice were great centers of art at this time.

In Northern Europe, several Flemish and German artists contributed greatly to the painting and art of this period. The most noted artists included Jan van Eyck, Hieronymus Bosch, Pieter Breughel, and Albrecht Durer.

Baroque Art

(1600 A.D. to 1700 A.D.)

Baroque art began in Rome in the first half of the sixteenth century. The Baroque artists developed a style of painting in which swirling figures and unusual compositions utilizing multicurved arrangements gave a feeling of super-reality as well as romantic mysticism to their compositions. Baroque art extended from Italy to Flanders, Holland, France, and Spain. In each of these countries, certain outstanding artists emerged. These included Peter Paul Rubens, El Greco, Velazquez, Frans Hals, Rembrandt, Vermeer, and Poussin.

Rococo Art

(1700 A.D. to 1789 A.D.)

Rococo art is usually considered a modification or domestication of the Baroque style. Its influence was felt in the entire western world. Rococo art was very decorative, gay, ornamental, and free. It was in fact a reflection of times which were relatively free from major world catastrophies and upheavals. Rococo art was present in France, Italy, Holland, and England. Although no great figures emerged during this flamboyant period in art, several artists made minor marks on the scene. These included Watteau and Fragonard in France, and Van Dyck, Holbein, Reynolds, Gainsborough and Hogarth in England. Rococo art was such a definite style that it was incorporated into everything possible from architecture, tapestries and teapot handles to furniture pieces and silverware. Its major influence ended about the time of the French Revolution of 1789.

Neoclassicism

Neoclassicism was the result in part of the French Revolution, whereby the new government wished their artistic voice to speak of good fortune to come. Rococo art, which spoke of the aristocracy, was buried and the new classical style began. The glory of Greece and Rome once again rose to the fore, and French artists adopted traditional styles in their search for a classical grace befitting the new regime. Strong emphasis was placed on technical skill and composition. Content was based on classical themes and heroic ideals. Human feeling became somewhat submerged due to the emphasis on style. Figures tend to be cold and intellectually treated. Paintings done during this period tend to have a sophisticated appearance, although technical rendition is superb. The most notable artists of this period include Jacques Louis David and Jean Auguste Dominique Ingres.

Romanticism

Romanticism was a revolt from the French Academy with its traditional classicism and imitative styles. It began around the time of the Salon of 1819. This type of painting style introduced human feelings back into the figures. The subjects tended to be highly exaggerated versions of life treated in a very idyllic manner. In France, Theodore Gericault and Eugene Delacroix were most influential in leading the Romantic movement in art. In America, Albert Ryder and George Inness painted in a manner that paralleled the Romantic manner.

Realism

Realism was a mid-nineteenth century form of art expression in which the subject was treated in a highly realistic manner. Realistic qualities in the paintings were achieved by using dramatic effects of light and dark and by exaggerating subjects for emphasis. These artists often painted social conditions which reflected economic struggles of the times. Some artists who could be included within this period include Honore Daumier, Francisco Goya, and Rembrandt van Rijn.

Impressionism

This art movement began in France about 1870 and was due in part to an interest of how natural light effects occur in nature. Artists of this school tried to achieve with pigment on canvas the

"Blind Hurdy Gurdy Player,"
oil, Pieter Brueghel the Elder.
Courtesy: Crocker Art Gallery,
Sacramento, California.

"Quiet Waters," etching, Lionel
Barrymore.
Courtesy: Crocker Art Gallery,
Sacramento, California.

Sometimes paintings shock and disturb us. At other times they reflect our point of view. Art as a force can alert us to personal strife, social conditions, and other human problems past and present.

"St. Eustice," engraving, Albrecht Durer.
Courtesy: Crocker Art Gallery,
Sacramento, California.

"The Judas Kiss," German, sixteenth century.
Courtesy: Crocker Art Gallery,
Sacramento, California.

"Owl"
by Donald W. Herberholz
Welded Metal Sculpture

"There, there Simba"
by Earl Linderman
Pastel

The artist as an interpreter of life registers the varying pulsebeats which come within his experiences. Each artist says what he feels in a personal style, often developing new symbols of communication in the process.

Courtesy of the artist

"Quiet Place"
by James Doerter
Watercolor

"Rooster"
by Paul Beckman
Print

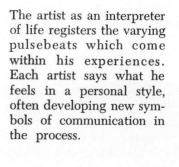

"Academic Priest"
by Bruce Carter
Print

same effect as one would receive while viewing fields and landscapes if bright sunlight were present. The Impressionist painters succeeded in developing new ways of mixing pigments, of organizing space in relation to color, and of intensifying their palette to a much greater degree than previously accepted standards permitted. Two very influential painters of this movement in art included Claude Monet and Auguste Renoir.

Post-Impressionism

Post-Impressionism, which began about 1880, was an attempt by several artists in France to extend beyond the then popular Impressionistic styles which certain artists had developed. The post-impressionists were not entirely satisfied with the principles set down by the impressionists and set out to prove or clarify them. While still retaining the spontaneity and freshness of the Impressionist style, the post-impressionists developed many new styles and approaches to painting. Seurat and Cézanne approached the idea of painting by using scientific means. To this day Cézanne is considered the father of modern painting. Two other painters of this style included Vincent Van Gogh and Paul Gauguin.

Cubism

Cubism, which began in Paris shortly after the turn of the century, is considered the beginning of the abstract art movement. The most notable artists to explore and originate the Cubistic styles included Pablo Picasso and George Braque. Fernand Leger and Juan Gris also painted in the Cubistic manner. In developing the Cubistic style, the artist reduced the forms of the picture to simplified geometrical elements which included spheres, cylinders, rectangles, and other irregular shapes. Cubism opened the door for artistic inventiveness and exploration that continues to influence contemporary art. It also marks the point where the artist begins to develop art forms for their own sake, thus narrowing the path of communication between the artist and the general public.[3]

----

[3]For further discussion, see John Cannaday's statements in *A History of Western Art*, by John Ives Sewall, New York: Holt, Rinehart and Winston, 1961, p. 890.

Expressionism

Expressionism developed principally in Germany and France and was a reaction to conditions immediately surrounding World War I. It was an art form in which the artist expressed his own emotional reaction to a specific subject. Subject matter was usually based on depressing and violent themes which dwelt on the morbid side of life. Color was treated very subjectively with little attempt to relate it within a more natural relationship. Several artistic groups composed the Expressionist movement. In Germany, three succcessive groups included *The Bridge, The Blue Riders*, and *The New Objectivity*. Several artists who contributed fine works within the Expressionist style include Kandinsky, Grosz, Kollwitz, Barlach, Ensor, and Munch.

Surrealism

Surrealism developed shortly after World War I and was a reaction to conditions prevailing at the time. Surrealism was fathered by a smaller movement known as *Dada*, which was a protest against society and tradition. The ridiculous, the irrational, and the bizarre were all stock in trade for both Dada and surrealism. While Dada flickered and vanished into the undercurrent of painting, surrealism picked up momentum on the strength of new findings in psychology by Freud and others. The subconscious and dream themes dominated Surrealist paintings. Highly realistic handling of content tended to give the viewer a deeper sense of reality. Among the painters connected in and around the Surrealist movement, the following artists gained prominence: Max Ernst, Kurt Schwitters, Paul Klee, Dali, Miro, and Tanguy.

American Scene Painters

In America during the first half of the twentieth century, several artists have depicted the American scene each in an individual manner. The back yard, the small town, the rural scene, the commonplace, and the ordinary became subject matter for these artists. While the reasons governing the types and styles of paintings varied from satirical reactions against cubism then popular in Europe to humor over homespun virtues, several artists made their mark on the Ameri-

"Closed Era"
by Jean Pratt
Woodblock Print

(Illustration for the Joseph Conrad novel, 'Youth")
Artist: Dewitt Jayne
Oil

The artist as interpreter uses art media in a manner which best expresses his ideas and experiences at any particular time.

"Transit"
by Walter Ball
Oil

can scene. They include John Sloan, Grant Wood, Charles Burchfield, Ben Shahn, and Edward Hopper. Of this group, Ben Shahn stands out as one of America's contemporary painters of social conditions.

Abstract-Expressionism

Abstract Expressionism developed in the United States during the period 1950 to 1960. It was a movement that encouraged free experimentation and search by applying unorthodox methods of painting a picture. In many instances, paintings of this movement were done by dripping, throwing, splashing, and literally scrubbing the pigment into the canvas. A representative image of an object was not a necessary intention. Paintings of this school reflected the inner expression of the artist in emotional form. The leading exponents of abstract expressionism include Jackson Pollack, Franz Kline, Hans Hoffman, and Willem de Kooning.

References

Anderson, Donald M., *Elements of Design,* New York: Holt, Rinehart and Winston, Inc., 1961.

Berry, Ana M., *First Book of Paintings,* New York: Franklin Watts, Inc., 1960.

Baldinger, Wallace S., *The Visual Arts,* New York: Henry Holt and Company, revised 1963.

Borrison, Mary Jo, *Let's Go To An Art Museum,* New York: G. P. Putnam's Sons, 1960.

Brown, Margaret Wise, *The House of a Hundred Windows,* New York: Harper and Bros., 1945.

Canaday, John, *Mainstreams of Modern Art,* New York: Henry Holt & Co., Inc., 1959.

Compton's Pictured Encyclopedia, Chicago: F. E. Compton and Co., 1963.

Conant, Howard, and Randall, Arne, *Art in Education,* Peoria, Ill.: Chas. A. Bennett, 1959.

de Barhegyi, Suzanne, *Museums,* New York: Holt, Rinehart & Winston, Inc., 1962.

Faulkner, R., Ziegfeld, E., and Hill G., *Art Today,* fourth edition, New York: Holt, Rinehart & Winston, Inc., 1963.

Field Enterprises Educational Corp., *World Book Encyclopedia,* Vol. 14, Chicago: Merchandise Mart Plaza, 1963.

Fleming, William, *Arts and Ideas,* (Revised Ed.) New York: Holt, Rinehart, Winston, 1963.

Flexner, James T., *Pocket History of American Painting,* New York: Washington Square Press, Inc., 1962.

Gardner, Helen, *Art Through the Ages,* (Third Ed.) New York: Harcourt, Brace and Co., 1960.

Hunt, C., and Carlson, B. W., *Masks and Mask Makers,* New York: Abingdon Press, 1961.

Hunter, Sam, *Modern French Painting,* New York: Dell Publishing Co., (paperback).

Janson, H. W., and D. J. Janson, *The Story of Painting,* New York: Harry N. Abrams, Inc., 1952.

Linderman, Earl W., "Let's Learn About Art," *Arts and Activities,* December, 1963.

Linderman, Earl W., "Appreciation Deserves An Early Start," *Arts and Activities,* October, 1962.

MacAgy, Douglas and Elizabeth, *Going for a Walk With a Line,* Garden City, New York: Doubleday & Co., 1959.

McCurdy, Charles, editor, *Modern Art: A Pictorial Anthology,* New York: Macmillian Co., 1958.

McDarrah, Fred W., *The Artist's World,* New York: E. P. Dutton and Co., Inc., 1961.

Mendelowitz, Daniel M., *A History of American Art,* New York: Holt, Rinehart & Winston, Inc., 1960.

Meyers, Bernard, *Understanding The Arts,* New York: Henry Holt and Company, revised 1963.

Moore, Lamont, *First Book of Paintings,* New York: Franklin Watts, Inc., 1960.

Ocvirk, Bone, Stinson, and Wigg, *Art Fundamentals,* Dubuque, Iowa: Wm. C. Brown Company Publishers, 1962.

O'Neill, Mary, *Hailstones and Halibut Bones,* Garden City, New York: Doubleday & Co., 1961.

Osmond, Edward, *Houses,* London: B. T. Botsford, Ltd., 1956.

Paschel, Herbert, *First Book of Color,* New York: Franklin Watts, Inc., 1959.

Seiberling, Frank, *Looking Into Art,* New York: Henry Holt & Co., 1959.

Sewall, John Ives, *A History of Western Art* (Revised Ed.), New York: Holt, Rinehart, Winston, 1963.

Simpson, Martha, *Art Is For Everyone,* New York: McGraw-Hill Co., 1951.

Taylor, Joshua C., *Learning To Look: A Handbook for the Visual Arts,* Chicago: University of Chicago Press, 1957.

Vale, Edmund, *Cathedrals,* London: B. T. Botsford, Ltd., 1957.

Vale, Edmund, *Churches,* London: B. T. Botsford, Ltd., 1954.

Wechsler, Herman J., *The Pocket Book of Old Masters,* New York: Washington Square Press, Inc., 1961.

Young, Mary, *Singing Windows,* New York: Abingdon Press, 1962.

Index